C000141998

# Islamic Concept of God

# Islamic Concept of God

Mohammad Zia Ullah

**KPI**

London, Boston and Henley

First published in 1984 by KPI Limited
14 Leicester Square, London WC2H 7PH, England

Reprinted with corrections and first published
as a paperback in 1985

Distributed by
Routledge & Kegan Paul plc
14 Leicester Square, London WC2H 7PH, England

Routledge & Kegan Paul Inc
9 Park Street, Boston, Mass. 02108, USA and

Routledge & Kegan Paul plc
Broadway House, Newtown Road,
Henley-on-Thames, Oxon RG9 1EN, England

Set in Baskerville 10/12pt by Input Typesetting Ltd, London
and printed in Great Britain by
St Edmundsbury Press, Bury St Edmunds, Suffolk

© Mohammad Zia Ullah 1984

No part of this book may be reproduced in
any form without permission from the publisher,
except for the quotation of brief passages in criticism

Library of Congress Cataloging in Publication Data
Zia Ullah, Mohammad.
Islamic concept of God.
Includes index.
1. God (Islam)    I. Title.
BP166.2.Z52    1983        297'.211        83-18417
ISBN 0-7103-0076-X (C)
ISBN 0-7103-0127-8 (Pbk)

To my father:

whose contact and living relationship with his Creator
was a moving example not only for me, his son,
but also for all those who came closest to him.

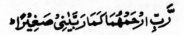

Lord, have mercy on my
father and my mother, even
as they cared for me and
ministered to my needs when
I was young (17:25).

اس درجہ ترقی خاک کو دی      وہ ہوش میں آکر شوق بنی

اس شوق کا خود منظورِ نظر      سُبحان اللہ ! سُبحان اللہ

This clay
hath He raised so high,
gifted it first with awareness
in quest of Himself.
All praise to Allah,
All glory to Allah.

# Contents

# Preface

The delights and excitements of the modern world leave little or no time for us to think of ultimate questions, like whence we came, whither we go, who has sent us into this world and to what end or purpose. But if now and then we spare our moments of solitude to think about these questions we will realize that to do so is only to our own benefit.

It is obvious that we have not come into being of our own accord, nor shall we depart from this life by our own choosing. Our coming and going are subject to the will of our Creator. Indifference to Him and to the purpose of our creation can, therefore, only work to our disadvantage. On the other hand, if we acquire knowledge and awareness about Him and fashion our lives in accordance with His will and design this will surely be a way to safety and peace. And precisely to this way of safety and peace Islam invites all mankind – the pivotal focus of which is Allah, our Creator. Our relationship with Him should be our major concern.

This book is an attempt to understand as well as to work out this relationship in daily life.

The Holy Quran presents our Creator as an all-powerful being, loving, compassionate and benevolent. He has created us only to shower His blessings on us. He Himself seeks nothing from His creatures. Being transcendent He is far and above such needs and desires. What use and what need has He for creatures made by Him out of clay as a manifestation of His great creative powers? Out of sheer grace has He endowed us with privilege of existence and set us on an unending course of progress and evolution – Himself being our final goal. Thus we read in the Holy Quran:

(i) then to your Lord will be your return (6:165).
(ii) and to Allah is the return (3:29).

(iii)  then to your Lord will you be brought back (32:12).
(iv)  who when a misfortune overtakes them, say, surely to Allah
       we belong and to Him shall we return (2:157).
 (v)  know for certain that they will meet their Lord and to Him
       will they return (2:47).
(vi)  thou, O man, art labouring toward thy Lord, a hard
       labouring; then thou art going to meet Him (84:7).

Stages of progress we have already covered. Was not there a
time when we were in the form of elements of which we are
compounded? But each succeeding stage is higher than the
previous one. Let us compare our present life, endowed as it is
with intelligence and many other faculties, with our condition in
the mother's womb. Is not the difference breathtaking,
maddening? This onward march ordained and decreed by our
merciful Creator promises to continue. Just as His grace and
splendour are infinite, so also is our spiritual journey in His
quest. No wonder, therefore, life hereafter is eternal.

He created us and vouchsafed to us the gift of reason so that
with its help we can understand and recognize Him. He also
decreed that communion with Him is the goal of our life. Our
Creator desires that we pursue the quickest path leading to Him.
And what could be and what actually is this path? Himself being
goodness personified, goodness in us will propel us to Him. Evil,
the opposite of good, is abhorrent to our Creator. Evil in us,
therefore, will drive us away from Him. The do's spelt out in the
Quran are nothing but details of actions leading us towards Him,
the don'ts, details of actions leading us away from Him. Those
who regard these commandments as arbitrary, prescribed by
God for his own pleasure and imposed without any rhyme or
reason are mistaken in the extreme. Just as the acquisition of
knowledge only redounds to the good of the person acquiring it,
so the life of virtue benefits the person treading the straight path.
In addition to the gift of reason our merciful Creator has also
endowed us with the power to distinguish between right and
wrong, good and evil. We read in the Quran:

And He revealed to it (the human soul) what is wrong for it

and what is right for it; he indeed prospers who purifies it and he is ruined who corrupts it (91.99–11).

With the help of this faculty commonly known as conscience, we are able to choose between good and evil and stay on the right path. Furthermore, planted deep within our nature is a seed of the avowal of our Creator's existence. We read in the Quran:

And when Thy Lord brings forth from Adam's children – out of their loins – their offspring and makes them witnesses against their own selves by saying: 'Am I not your Lord?' they say, 'Yes, we do bear witness.' (7:173)

This verse points to our innate nature which contains the sacred seed of the Almighty's love and avowal to which every normal person will bear witness. But like all other seeds this seed also requires food and nourishment. And this is what this book attempts to do. If the author's effort, in the eyes of the reader, has achieved this purpose he may breathe a prayer for him. If, on the other hand, the reader finds any deficiencies he should act with forbearance. To err is human and no man is free from this human failing.

# I

ہے قیدِ آب و خاک سے باہر مقامِ دل
مانا خمیرِ مایہ میرا ماء و طین ہے

The heart's station
is far away,
not in this dungeon
of dust and damp.
True, its origin is humble–
water only and mortal clay.

The basic values of modern civilization are purely materialistic. Its widespread evil influences permeate everywhere. As a result all religious truths are denied and religion is held in ridicule. The central point in religious faith is the being and person of God. But God is dismissed as an invention of the human mind. Man, it is said, invented gods and goddesses during the days of his infancy and ignorance. Thus, conception of God is an extension of the same infantile attitude of mind and amounts to no more than saying after Copernicus that the sun moves round the earth. But the truth is that belief in God is one of the natural dispositions of man. It is not a question requiring any subtlety of logical argumentation. Says God in the Holy Quran.

وَفِي الْأَرْضِ آيَاتٌ لِّلْمُوقِنِينَ ۝ وَفِي أَنفُسِكُمْ ۚ أَفَلَا تُبْصِرُونَ ۝

And in the earth are Signs for those who have *certainty* of faith. And also in your own selves. Will you not then see? (51:21, 22)

There is evidence galore only if man would occasionally withdraw into solitude and contemplate with an unprejudiced mind. Did he come to birth of himself? Is he his own Creator?

Who will say 'Yes' to such questions? So much will be obvious to anyone who consults his own conscience. No, his conscience will say. Then, if man is not his own creator, the Creator has to be someone else, outside of him. Could it be his parents? No, again. For, what is true of one man is true *ipso facto* of his parents. Man, in short, is himself proof of the existence of God. Beautifully has Akbar Allahabadi expressed the idea in a couplet:

مری ہستی ہے خود شاہدِ وجودِ ذاتِ باری کی

دلیل ایسی ہے یہ جو عمر بھر ردّ ہو نہیں سکتی

> My existence
> is witness
> to the existence of God.
> The proof is irrefutable –
> you may try and refute it,
> all your life.

And Maulana Rumi similarly in his *Mathnavi* – in elegant verse:

جنبشِ ما ہر دمے خود اشہدست

کہ گواہِ ذوالجلال سرمدست

گردشِ سنگ آسیا در اضطراب

اشہد آمد بر وجودِ جوئے آب

> The movements I make
> are proof very strong,
> that God Al-mighty,
> Everlasting,
> there certainly is.

> Same as the stone of the water-mill,
> as it moves,
> proves a stream of water
> there certainly is.

All our little movements throughout our life are witness sure of the existence of the God of might and power, the God eternal. Just as the millstone of the water-mill is proof of the running stream of water. So is my life – and every movement of my life – proof of the existence and power of God. The water-mill will not run without a running stream. Nor will life pulsate in me without the eternal and powerful Lord of Life.

Similarly the Quran bears witness to the sacred covenant between mankind and its creator:

وَإِذْ أَخَذَ رَبُّكَ مِنْ بَنِيٓ ادَمَ مِنْ ظُهُورِهِمْ ذُرِّيَّتَهُمْ وَأَشْهَدَهُمْ عَلَىٰٓ أَنْفُسِهِمْ أَلَسْتُ بِرَبِّكُمْ قَالُوا بَلَىٰ

And when thy Lord brings forth from Adam's children – out of their loins – their offspring and makes them witnesses against their own selves by saying: Am I not your Lord? they say, 'Yes, we do bear witness' (7:173).

To a sane person, this covenant is undeniable evidence of the existence of the great Creator. Planted in man's nature is the vital seed of the Almighty's love and avowal of His existence. The seed needs life – giving sustenance to flourish and flower, and, unless denied this sustenance by a polluted environment, it remains a constant and continuous guide to the Lord, and the nature of man ever keeps proclaiming, irresistibly, at all times and all places, 'Yes, yes, we are witness to Thy creation.'

دلِ ازل سے ہے کوئی آج کا شیدائی ہے
تھی جو اک چوٹ پُرانی وہ اُبھر آئی ہے

This quest of the heart
is old and eternal:
you think it started today?
No, the blow came long ago,
it has shown up again today.

And in the words of Rumi:

نافِ ما بر مہرِ خود ببریدہ اند          عشقِ خود در جانِ ما کاریدہ اند

My navel-cord was cut
with promise of Thy love
for me:
and in my nature didst Thou sow
the seed of my love
for Thee.

My birth is witness of my Creator. My origin divine is in my
seed, in my nature. It is the poisonous winds of materialism
which blow over this seed and destroy it. No wonder so many
today find themselves helpless, unable to raise their heads from
under the filth of doubt which covers them. That is precisely
what has happened to modern man and the modern world. Has
not the poet said:

اور تو سب کچھ ان کی بزم میں ہے          اِک خُدا ہی نظر نہیں آتا

One thing in this circle,
not mentioned, not discussed,
is God, poor God:
everything else is.

Alas the terrifying stresses of modern materialism have buried the sacred seed of the Almighty's love and avowal of His existence deep beneath a heavy weight of moral decay. But without these corrupting materialistic influences the existence of the Supreme Being remains the great, the ever-present and eternal truth. Compared to this truth nothing else could be more true, more real. Everything else but He would be as naught. Because everything would then be a manifestation, a sign, or a proof of Him. We know sunshine and we know shade. But could there be sunlight without the sun or shade without the tree?

سُنو! آتی ہے ہر طرف سے صدا

کہ باطل ہے ہر چیز حق کے سوا

Hark, and listen with care –
you'll hear it whispered
from every side, from everywhere –
'Empty and fleeting is everything except God.'

But it is not our own nature only that speaks. There are other proofs, other evidences and logical arguments which speak of God's existence. It is surprising how people can ignore these proofs, these evidences. Let us look at science.

Let us try and see what science has to say about this vast universe and about its tiniest particles, all witnesses of their Creator.

ہر دم از کارِخ عالم آدازلیست    کریکش بانی و بنا سازلیست

ایں جہاں را عمارت اندازلیست    و از جہاں بر تراست ومتنازلیست

Every moment
proclaims
there is someone –
who made this ordered world

and fashioned it too –
and having made it to a measure,
raised Himself above,
ever to remain apart
from His creation.

# II

This whole world of matter and life is eloquent testimony of the fact that it has had a Creator, a designer. Let us first take man, whose creation and whose body are a miracle most amazing. The libraries of anatomy and allied human sciences are full of the details of this miracle, but we may refer to a few here. The lone journey of life starts from humble beginnings, when one microscopic cell joins with another in the darkness of the mother's womb. Beginning in such small narrow confines the saga of its growth after it leaves the mother's womb makes a breath-taking story of wonder upon wonder before which the tales of the Arabian Nights pale into nothingness. See how this insignificant cell, without any knowledge of its own, grows into a complete human being within its allotted time. How it first develops its perfect but lifeless body, and then when its time for quickening is reached, it becomes a living creature inside its mother's womb. 'You were lifeless but He made you come alive' is the apt Quranic description. Says the Holy Quran:

كُنْتُمْ أَمْوَاتًا فَأَحْيَاكُمْ

You were without life, He gave you life (2:29).

Those who deny there is any life after death, let them ponder at this cryptic description by the Holy Quran of how life begins to pulsate in dead matter. They were a dead mass at one time. God breathed life into them. What has happened once to them already should not be a cause of surprise if it happens again. Why wonder?

And there is further cause for wonder when we see the development of this lifeless body occupying a mere few inches in its mother's womb. It is developing these very powers and qualities which it will need in the existence and vast universe which await it at its birth. It is unaware of the grand journey on which it is embarked, and yet it is most appropriately equipping itself for that very journey. It is so tiny that you can see it only with a microscope, but hidden in it is the full range of all human organs and each of those human organs is complex beyond any man-made machine. Surpassing them all is the human brain, to which no comparable machine has been or will ever be built. It is in a class by itself, as it possesses the non-material powers of reason and intellect. These powers enable man to make unlimited progress until he can leave his earthly abode and land on the moon. It is a breath-taking thought that early man dwelt in caves and today he plans to colonize outer space and heavenly bodies. At one time man's highest reach was to make stone implements; today he controls the limitless energy of the atom. This ability of his brain to convert the material into non-material is man's crowning glory. The humble loaf of bread which sustains the philosopher, is it not the source of his wisdom? If the philosopher had not received this nourishment, would we not have been deprived of his philosophy?

Here is something that those who are wedded to reason and deny the existence of the soul should ponder. Reason is non-material in its essence; how can it have any connection with man's food and with his brain? That would be a connection between what is material and what is non-material and they themselves deny this possibility. This is their main argument for denying the existence of the soul. The more we reflect the more miraculous seem man's creation, man's body and man's achievements. Could all this have come about of itself and with no-one looking after?

چل رہی ہے جس سے جسمانی مشین

کوئی پوشیدہ کسانی اور ہے

This body-machine
that keeps ticking cannot do this:
not without a lever
hidden somewhere.

# III

Now have a look at the wide world, this cosmos that lies beside and outside of man. The earth we live on rotates round its axis every twenty-four hours. And this rotation results in the alternation of day and night for us, that we may work during the day and rest during the night. Then the earth revolves round the sun once every one year. And this annual revolution gives us our four seasons each year, summer, winter, spring, autumn. Besides giving us our four seasons the annual revolution of the earth round the sun also gives us our crops, foods and fruits of different kinds. At the same time, let us remember that this earth of ours, this globe with its well-peopled lands, its skyscrapers, its mountains, its mines rich with minerals, its plains, oceans and all that they hold, is ever on the move at the terrific speed of 684,000 miles per hour. This movement we never become aware of. It is as though there was no movement. If science had not found this out, we would have continued to think the earth was standing still, as still as a stone. Just think how much it takes to move a small weight from one place to another. Or how much it takes to move an object that is lying still and then to keep it in constant motion? From this you can form some idea of the vast amount of energy it must take to keep in constant motion not only the earth but also a countless number of other planets. God only knows for how long they have been coursing this limitless space. What power, what strength must the Divine Hand have that maintains these motions.

Now turn to the heavenly bodies that keep coursing in their appointed orbits in space, with a precision unmatched by the most precise time-keepers made by man. The best of such time-keepers lose or gain at least a few seconds every week. These errors have then to be corrected by chronometers installed in observatories to note the time of the revolutions of heavenly bodies. This is made possible by a supreme order, by a system of laws which rules the entire universe. But from where came these laws, this order? Of themselves, would you say? And how senseless would this be? Would reason endorse a thought as senseless as that?

Let us recall a denier of God who became engaged in argument with a believer, how he lost the argument to his shame? The believer had given all sorts of arguments, but to no avail. One day, at last, he purchased a globe from a store of school apparatus. The disbelieving friend came to see him in his study. Finding something new with the believer he asked, who had made this globe and placed it where it was? The believer replied in jest, it had made itself and moved into his study! The disbeliever said he was not such a fool as to think so.

The argument over God started again. A small globe, part of a normal school apparatus, cannot create itself, so how can the very big globe, our earth? How can the countless other planets, infinitely bigger than our earth? And yet they are all held aloft in perfect co-ordination in the heavens, by laws which are so extraordinary, they never make a mistake.

فَاطِرُ السَّمٰوٰتِ وَالْأَرْضِ

He is God, Creator, Originator of the Heavens and the earth (42:12).

Science presents us with only a faint picture of the design, the wisdom, the architectural genius evident in the heavens and the earth. Yet read about it and you will find yourself lost in amazement and wonder. Our earth is but a small, tiny and insignificant speck in the whole universe. What there is besides it in space is so infinite, so awful, you cannot but endorse what is said in the verse:

اے خداوندِ خلق و عالمیاں          خلق و عالم زقدرتت حیراں

چہ مہیب است شانِ شوکتِ تو          چہ عجیب است کار و صنعتِ تو

Lord of the worlds,
Lord of all creation!
Thy creatures, Thy worlds,
astonished all
at Thy power.

Great Thy Glory
and great Thy Grandeur,
wondrous Thy handiwork.

We are in the dark at night. Or we tremble with cold. We
make a light to see what is around us. Or a fire to warm ourselves.
But the light reaches only a few yards around and the fire we
make is but limited. Compare with this the light and heat of the
sun. The difference is maddening. The sun, the heavenly sun,
emits both light and heat. Not for any limited space, but for all
the worlds. With unfailing, astounding perfection. Billions and
billions of years have passed and there is no slackening in either
its heat or its light. The sun is a furnace on fire, kept alive by
an unending series of atomic explosions. No fuel has to be
imported by it from outside. It produces its own fuel, its own
fire, to warm the worlds around and to keep them in lustre.

The vast immeasurable dimensions of space within which the
heavenly bodies carry on their appointed tasks leave us spell-
bound. Their numbers are beyond count. It is easier to count
the particles of sand on all the sea-shores of the world. Not the
numbers of heavenly bodies. Are you afraid of congestion in
space? But no, even congestion is taken care of. So vast is our
space, the infinite numbers of our planets make no difference to
it. There is room for ever more. Space still seems empty. Three
wasps flying over the whole of Europe will not take as much
room as all the heavenly bodies taken together. And the distances
between them? They are so great the human mind cannot
comprehend them. They are not to be measured in miles. Scien-

tists have invented the measure of light years for these distances. Light travels at the rate of 186,000 miles per second. A light ray girdles our earth seven times in a second. In one year it will have travelled 186,000 × 60 × 60 × 24 × 365 miles. This gives us the measure of one light year. And the scientists tell us that some heavenly bodies are at a distance of 10,000 million light years from us. This is stunning for human comprehension.

The light of the sun takes eight minutes to reach us. But from the star Betelgeux it takes one hundred years. The diameter of this star is 273,000,000 miles, three times longer than the distance between our earth and the sun. And it is small – very small – compared with other stars. Some of these have diameters more than 1,000,000,000 miles. There are many stars, such as Cepheids, which are more than 60,000 times as luminous as our sun.

Then our solar system is not unique. Myriad other such systems are hurtling through space. And outside the galaxy, of which our solar system is a small part, is an unending system of galaxies and island universes compared to which our galaxy is but a speck of dust. Every increase in the power of our telescopes reveals an ever-increasing population of previously unseen island universes, and this unending process continues to unfold further and further. It seems that all that the scientists and the astronomers have discovered in the unplumbed depths of space is only a preliminary and misty view of the grand reality. Anyone who ponders at the magnificent works of the great Creator will be filled with an overpowering sense of humility; and from the depths of his soul will go up a spontaneous cry that 'Allah is the Greatest.' This is the emotion described thus by the Quran:

اِنَّمَا يُؤْمِنُ بِاٰيٰتِنَا الَّذِيْنَ اِذَا ذُكِّرُوْا بِهَا خَرُّوْا سُجَّدًا وَّسَبَّحُوْا بِحَمْدِ رَبِّهِمْ وَهُمْ لَا يَسْتَكْبِرُوْنَ ۩

Only they believe in our signs who, when they are reminded of them, fall down prostrate and celebrate the praises of their Lord, and they are not proud (3:134).

But woe for the intellect that goes astray, and which turns away from the Great Creator and insists on puerile debate and argument. This spiritual blindness is aptly depicted by the Quran:

قَالَتْ رُسُلُهُمْ اَفِى اللّٰهِ شَكٌّ فَاطِرِ السَّمٰوٰتِ وَالْاَرْضِ

Their Messengers said, 'Are you in doubt concerning Allah, Maker of the heavens and the earth?' (14:11)

The spiritual myopia of man could not have a more eloquent description. And

ہر چیز میں خدا کی ضیا کا ظہور ہے
پر پھر بھی غافلوں سے وُہ دلدار دُور ہے

Everything great, everything small
is resplendent with the Light of God,
but those who are neglectful
can't discern the Beloved still.

Newton, the famous scientist, was the first to observe the laws which regulate the motions of heavenly bodies. As a result he could not help proclaiming that this vast physical universe is only a pointer to the might, power and glory of Him who created it. And He is eternal and everywhere. And after creating it, He has not retired to rest. He continues to rule His creation. And so perfect is His control that our power over our own bodies, our senses, our muscles, is insignificant when compared with His control over His Creation.

# IV

Let us now turn our attention from the frightening and mighty world of the far-flung heavens, to that other world where everything is exceedingly small. This is the world of tiny particles, invisible even to the keenest eye, and yet endowed with the most wonderful properties. Man himself falls almost half-way in the scale of magnitude between these tiny particles and the stars in the massive galaxies. The microbe is invisible without the help of a microscope and yet it shows the miraculous cycles of life and death, of spread and decay in health and disease, in a hundred different facets of human existence. Here lies a vast unfathomed ocean of knowledge in which we continue to find ever-new nuggets of knowledge as we dive to greater and deeper depths.

# V

Modern research into the constitution of the atom has revealed many astonishing phenomena. The most solid ordinary object is not really what it appears to the eyes; at work in it is a mysterious universe. Look at the kettle bubbling on the hearth giving out wisps of steam; are its particles in motion or at rest? Surely, the kettle is solid metal, its particles must be at rest, even though the steam may be moving. If you rely on your eyes that is what you would say, but you would be wrong, according to scientific evidence. The parts of metal of which the kettle is made are themselves nothing but collections of electrons and protons. The electrons are in perpetual motion around their nuclei, the protons at the terrific speed of 100,000,000,000,000 revolutions or more per second. Science has entered into the heart of the atom and found the old view no longer tenable that matter is only a collection of small solid particles. Now the language used by science is electrons and protons. The atom – the so-called last particle of matter – is a system of electrons and protons in perpetual motion. Each atom, therefore is itself a kind of planetary system, similar to our solar system. In the solar system the planets revolve round their centre, the sun. So in the atom the electrons keep revolving round the protons, their nuclei. We cannot see the atom. But science has peeped into it by indirect methods. It has even determined the speed with which the electrons revolve round the protons. It is said that the space in which these movements take place is as tiny as could be – about one-millionth of a square inch. This is staggering. In our solar system we have the planets moving in incredibly *expansive* space round the sun. And in the atom, in an incredibly *small* and limited space, we have the electrons moving round the protons. Thus we have two similar systems in the world of matter, one in the expansive, unlimited space around us, the other in the incredibly confined and limited world of the atoms. The similarity is complete. In the solar system the planets which move round the sun remain at a distance from the sun. So in the atom the electrons keep their distance from the nucleus. A well-built, 6-foot heavyweight, about 240 pounds, could be pressed hard, so as to abolish all spaces between the electrons and protons of the particles of his body, and became tight-packed into one small body. The size of this body would become so reduced, you could not see it except with the help of an electro-microscope. Science has found out a great deal about the ultimate particles of matter. Yet not enough. But from what it has found out it seems that in these infinitesimally small particles of matter, nature has stored immeasurable treasures of energy. The world only waits for man to get hold of these hidden treasures of energy and further change the face of the world.

As an illustration take a piece of coal of the size of a peanut. According to modern science there is sufficient atomic energy in this piece of coal, enough to propel an ocean-liner with several thousand passengers on board, a first-class hotel and other amenities from England to America and back. Similarly if you could tap a pound of coal for the atomic energy it contains, sufficient energy would be found in it to run all the industries of England for fifteen days.

کیا عجب تُو نے ہر ایک ذرّہ میں رکھے ہیں خواص
کون پڑھ سکتا ہے سارا دفترِ اِن اَسرار کا

On the meanest particle
Thou hast endowed
properties so amazing –
who can discern
and who can narrate
the secrets of them all?

## VI

In short we are left gaping in wonder whether we look at a particle of dust or at a big heavenly body coursing in space. Both bear the same miraculous stamp, pointing to one and the same Creator.

ہے عجب جلوہ تری قدرت کا پیارے ہر طرف

جس طرف دیکھیں وہی راہ ہے ترے دیدار کا

> So strange, diverse,
> in all directions scattered,
> O dear Lord
> is Thy power.
> Should we but look –
> around, above, below –
> every time we view some aspect of Thee.

But if you have said goodbye to your natural understanding and your conscience, if you have acquired spiritual myopia you cannot see the truth of God's existence writ large in all nature. Truly has the poet Akbar depicted the situation:

ذہن میں جو گھر گیا لاانتہا کیوں کر ہُوا

جو سمجھ میں آگیا پھر وہ خدا کیوں کر ہُوا

> If the mind can contain it
> and the intellect comprehend it –
> how can it be God,
> the God that is infinite?

God is infinite, pervasive, and man finite and limited to a locality. Man cannot comprehend God as he can other things. To expect this is wrong. God is without limits, without dimensions. We would be fools to ask for Him to step down from His throne of infinite attributes to become comprehensible for us. How can a limitless, infinite being be contained in the mind of a limited being like man?

بریں عقل و دانش باید گریست

Woe to this logic
and this understanding!

# VII

Such in short is our God, our Creator, our Lord.

فَذَٰلِكُمُ اللَّهُ رَبُّكُمُ الْحَقُّ

Such is Allah, your True Lord (10:33).

All religions have taught about Him. It is Him they have urged men to know and to love. It is He Who has been the centre of their teaching, their message. True, they have taught in the main two kinds of duties, duties we owe to God and duties we owe to fellow men. But these duties have one great end in view, and that is God.

Duties we owe to God are prescribed, so that we can get nearer and nearer to Him. Duties we owe to fellow men have the same end in view. For, when we serve our fellow men we please our God and get closer to Him. In a sense, creatures of God are God's children. If we show love and affection to children – lift one to our lap and give a sweet to another – will it not please their parents? Will they not wish to show love and affection to you? So it is with God.

But for the moment we are not concerned so much with our duties to men. Therefore, we will deal rather with the duties we owe to God. And dealing with this subject every religion including Islam has laid special stress on two points.

Firstly, that in our faith we should associate no-one else with Him.

Secondly, we must love God more than anyone else.

It is a pity that with the passage of time Muslims also, like the followers of other religions, have mixed other things with the truth about God. Worship of tombs, of dead or hereditary saints goes on side by side with indifference to this our primary duty

– to love God. Dividing our belief in one God with belief in other gods is prohibited because greater deviation from the true and straight path there could not be. This is disloyalty to God, *Shirk* in Islamic parlance. For one who has yet to find the object of true belief, the question of getting close to God does not arise. *Shirk* (associating other deities with the one God) is also self-degrading. Man has been created to subjugate, to use and to rule other things. Could he bow in obeisance to these things? It is unthinkable.

The duty to love God more than anyone else is because God is the only one to Whom we really owe our love. There are Muslims who think love of God is not love of one like ourselves. Therefore, it is not natural. There are others who think that love of God makes a man indifferent to his other obligations. including the obligation to develop and put to use his other capacities. Love of God is enjoined in Islam, it is true. But it only means submission to Him and carrying out His ordinances. Between these two extreme groups there is a third group consisting of the great majority, engrossed in the affairs of the world, earning their living so exclusively that they have little or no time for anything outside their mundane interests. As Maulana Rumi has said:

عامہ راز عشق ہم خواجہ طبق
کے بود پروائے عشق صنع حق

Common folks
who eat and drink
and are happy
in their family circles –
how can they think
of loving God
for all He does for us?

# VIII

It is very much to the point, therefore, to inquire into the subject of love and try and see why no-one is as deserving of our love and devotion as is God, and why we cannot hope to achieve real and lasting satisfaction in love given to any other being.

The first question we like to put to the sceptics is, are they not acquainted with love as an experience? Or, are they complete strangers to it? Is it not a fact that the human heart is capable of love of many different kinds? Love of parents, love of one's children, love of near relations, love of riches, love of popularity, of a good name, love of power, of ruling others, love of one's country, love of knowledge and so on? Is not history – in the broadest sense – a history of this one human emotion? If this is true, is it not unfortunate and odd in the extreme, that the Being, the one Being to Whom we owe our birth and our growth, to love Whom is a guarantee of our welfare in life here and life hereafter, is considered by some to be inappropriate as an object of love?

لیک چشم دیدنت تو باز نیست
زین دلِ تو محرمِ این راز نیست

Your inward eye
never opens –
no wonder, therefore,
the secret remains hidden
from your heart.

On somewhat deeper reflection, the first thing we become

clearly aware of is that love of God – our Creator – is embedded
in human nature. It is part of the seed.

دل نمی گیرد تسلّی جُز خدا          ایں چنیں افتاد فطرت را ابتدا

> Satisfaction the heart can never achieve:
> not without God,
> and this has been the nature of man,
> from eternity.

In short, man can find no peace of mind without God's love. This
is a basic human instinct, even though, lured by the pleasures of
the flesh, one may crush this sacred seed rather than nourish it.
Like any ordinary seed, it must receive the necessary shelter and
nourishment, if it is to grow and develop. None the less, love for
his Creator is an inborn human instinct. This is an eternal truth,
even though some misguided persons may prevent this instinct
and try to satisfy their spiritual longing in the love and worship
of idols and false gods. The Holy Quran warns man about this:

مَثَلُ الَّذِيْنَ اتَّخَذُوْا مِنْ دُوْنِ اللّٰهِ اَوْلِيَآءَ كَمَثَلِ الْعَنْكَبُوْتِ ۖ اتَّخَذَتْ
بَيْتًا ۖ وَاِنَّ اَوْهَنَ الْبُيُوْتِ لَبَيْتُ الْعَنْكَبُوْتِ ۘ لَوْ كَانُوْا يَعْلَمُوْنَ ه

Worshippers of false Gods choose a home for their natural
disposition to love the One True God. But the home they
choose is – as the spider's web – the most fragile of all homes.
Would that they knew! (29:42)

Further, the purpose of human life has been made clear in the
divine revelation in the Quran in the clearest possible terms in
the following verse:

وَمَا خَلَقْتُ الْجِنَّ وَالْاِنْسَ اِلَّا لِيَعْبُدُوْنِ ه

And I have not created the jinn and the men but that they
should worship Me (51:57).

It would thus be unworthy of His greatness that He should have created us for a particular purpose and not have provided everything necessary for attaining it. The purpose of our lives is communion with our Creator, through worshipping Him, and by casting ourselves in the mould of His attributes. It is not possible that our lives would have a God-given purpose and yet not have been endowed with all the qualities necessary for fulfilling that divine destiny. The first step towards attaining any worthy goal is the desire and strong yearning for it in one's heart. It is precisely for this reason that love of God, the Creator, is part of man's natural endowment and therefore every true soul has an inborn yearning and desire for the loftiest of all human goals: communion with God. And how could it be otherwise when the ultimate human destiny is a return to the Lord to which Quran bears repeated witness thus:

$$اِنَّا اِلَيْهِ رَاجِعُوْنَ$$

To Him we are destined to return (2: 156).

$$ثُمَّ اِلٰى رَبِّكُمْ مَرْجِعُكُمْ$$

Then to your Lord will be your return (6:165).

$$وَ اِلَى اللّٰهِ الْمَصِيْرُ$$

And to Allah is the returning (3:28).

$$ثُمَّ اِلٰى رَبِّكُمْ تُرْجَعُوْنَ$$

Then to your Lord will you be brought back (32:12).

$$يہيچ آگهى نہ بود ز عشق و وفا مرا        خود ريختى متاعِ محبّت بدامنم$$

Nothing did I know,
of love or loyalty:
this precious gift,

out of sheer Grace,
gavest Thou to me.

The mystic acknowledges that he knew naught of love and devotion until these treasures were placed in his heart through divine grace. The human heart will not achieve the satisfaction, the delight it seeks, without contemplation, without worship, worship of our Creator. Worship is not a penalty we must pay. He has no need of our devotion, our praises, our obeisance. It is we who need this for our own inner solace and peace as well as to purify ourselves for the path that leads to Him. How very correctly does the Quran depict this condition of the human heart thus:

$$ اَلَا بِذِكْرِ اللهِ تَطْمَئِنُّ الْقُلُوْبُ $$

Aye! it is in the remembrance of Allah that hearts will find comfort (13:29).

Who can deny that the secret of genuine happiness and true peace of mind lies in anything else except the constant remembrance and worship of the Creator? Worship is not an affliction or an imposition, for God does not have the slightest need for it. He does not depend on us for His praise and glorification. We need to praise and glorify Him for our own spiritual purification. We know that every earthly abode needs a lamp to give it light: so does divine worship illuminate our soul.

$$ ہر سرائے را چراغے ہست صائب در جہاں $$
$$ سینہ و دل روشن از نُورِ عبادت می شود $$

Every house in this world
needs a light –
to dispel the dark at night.
So our hearts and souls do need
the light of worship –

to dispel the dark within.

It is an undeniable truth that even the largest measures of worldly success, material wealth, kingly power, personal glory and fame cannot by themselves lead to true happiness and genuine peace of mind. These blessings are vouchsafed only to the soul which has attained communion with its Creator through love, devotion and worship. This is indeed as it should be since the human heart was destined to be a throne for the Lord of the universe and no-one else.

نہ ہو طغیانِ مشتاقی تو میں رہتا نہیں باقی

کہ میری زندگی کیا ہے یہی طغیانِ مشتاقی

The billowing excitement of Love conjures life in me; with that gone I am no more.

# IX

Now let us attempt a certain amount of analysis. Love has its motives, its springs. We can name four such springs at once:

1 Beauty.
2 Beneficence.
3 Perfection.
4 Love of oneself or realization of oneself.

Let us consider these four springs of love, four motives, in turn, also where each would lead us by its own logic, through steps which naturally follow from it.

Is it God our Lord ultimately Whom we really should seek or something or someone else? If the answer is God, then the three groups mentioned before have lost the straight path and have moved away in wrong directions.

# X

The first thing that moves man to love is beauty. Beauty attracts. Its appreciation is part of the nature of man. It is impossible that there should be beauty and it should not move us. It is not different from our other senses, from taste, for instance. We distinguish between things sweet and things bitter. We feel attracted towards the former and turn away from the latter, so we feel attracted to beautiful objects and turn away from objects that are ugly. Beauty may be anywhere, in human beings, in external nature. Wherever it is, in whatever object it may be, it shows itself in its effects on us. Green landscapes and springs of water – who will not be delighted by them? Beautiful faces – who will not be pleased to see them? But where does the beauty of beautiful things come from? Who has created this beauty? Not self-created, for sure. It is created by God our Creator. And He Who has created all this beauty, how very beautiful must be He Himself. The beauty we find in the world around us is proof perfect of the unique, unequalled beauty of our Creator. It does not make good logic that He should be able to create beauty but Himself remain devoid of it. He Who gives beauty to others, how can He be without it Himself? Who enriches others must be rich Himself. He Who has nothing Himself, what can he give to others?

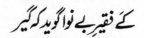

Surprising! a penniless beggar offering charity.

Beautiful things around us attract. Impossible that God, who lends beauty to everything else should not.

حُسنِ تو غِنی کند ز هرحُسن     مہرِ تو بحُود کُشد ز ہر یار

حُسنِ نمکینت ار نہ بُودے     از حُسنِ تو نہ بودے ہیچ آثار

شوخی ز تو یافت روئے خُوباں     رنگ از تو گرفت گُل بگُلزار

سیمیں ذقناں کہ سیب دارند     آمد ز ہماں بلند اشجار

ایں ہر دو ازاں دیار آئند

گیسوئے بتان و مشکِ تاتار

Thy Beauty makes us forget
all other beauties;
Thy grace makes us forget
those nearest and dearest to us.
But for Thy animating Beauty,
there would have been
no beauty –
Anywhere in the world.
The enchantment of beautiful faces
comes all from Thee;
the colour of flowers in each garden
also comes from Thee.
The apple-pink on white chins
comes
from the same
tall trees

And from the same lands
come these two –
the tresses of beautiful maidens
and the musk of Tartar.

This eternal beauty, even a passing view of it could inspire
verses like the following:

بن رہا ہے سارا عالم آئینۂ ابصار کا * کس قدر ظاہر ہے نور اس مبدأ الانوار کا

کیونکہ کچھ کچھ تھا نشاں اس میں جمالِ یار کا * چاند کو کل دیکھ کر میں سخت بے کل ہو گیا

مت کرو کچھ ذکر ہم سے ترک یا تاتار کا * اس بہار حسن کا دل میں ہمارے جوش ہے

ہر ستارے میں تماشہ ہے تری چمکار کا * چشمۂ خورشید میں موجیں تری مشہود ہیں

ہر گل گلشن میں ہے رنگ اس تری گلزار کا * خوبرویوں میں ملاحت ہے ترے اس حسن کی

ہاتھ ہے تری طرف ہر گیسوئے خمدار کا * چشم مستِ ہر حسیں ہر دم دکھاتی ہے تجھے

Patent and pervasive
Is this Light of Lights!
The whole world has become
one large mirror
for the willing to see.
Yesternight the moon I saw,
made me lose my peace –
for something in it resembled
the Beauty of the One
loved by me.
Its beauty abundant
has filled my heart
with frenzied joy – therefore
Tell me not of Tartar
or the Turkish beauty
The waves in this ocean, the sun,
are witness unto Thee.
Each scintillating star is a scene
of radiance
that's Thee.
The beauty of all beauties
of this world,
is Beauty Thine –
the rose, the rose garden, receive their colour

from the garden that's Thee.
The heavy-lidded eye of every beauty
reveals only Thee:
the curved lock on every cheek
has its hand
pointing to Thee.

Or see how sight of the fourteenth Moon can stimulate a whole
night of contemplation:

شب بھر رہا چرچا ترا       کل چودھویں کی رات تھی
کچھ نے کہا یہ چاند ہے       کچھ نے کہا چہرہ ترا

'Twas the night of the full moon.
You were the subject of discourse the
whole night.
Some said 'twas the moon they saw
some said 'twas Thee.

If we have a sensitive heart inside us, we must have experiences
similar to this:

جس کے سینے میں دلِ آگاہ ہے
اُس کے لب پر اللہ ہی اللہ ہے

He who has a perceiving heart
will have 'Allah, Allah', only
spring to his lips.

It is possible that on account of his own insensitive mind a
person may not feel the impact of beauty when in its presence –
the same as animals would remain unmoved by it. Likewise his
own lack of spiritual insight may not permit him to discern in
earthly beauty a pointer to the beauty divine, eternal, everlasting,

the ultimate source of all other beauty – ephemeral and fleeting,
though, essentially in character. But it is an undeniable truth
that beauty and love are connected naturally and eternally.
Where there is beauty there must be love. And nothing is more
beautiful than Allah.

اِک عکسِ ناتمام پہ عالم کو وجد ہے
کیا پُوچھنا ہے آپ کے حُسنِ و جمال کا

> It's a partial view we have,
> yet a whole world is in ecstasy;
> how would it be
> if we were granted
> a sight of Him,
> in His beauteous entirety!

If He were to momentarily unveil Himself, and manifest a
glimpse of His sublime beauty, all creation would be stunned
prostrate before His overpowering majesty: we cannot see Him
with our earthly eyes, for He is infinite and subtle, and we are
sordid and material, and the material cannot comprehend the
subtle.

وہ اپنے حُسن کی مستی سے ہیں مجبور پیدائی
مری آنکھوں کی بینائی میں ہیں اسبابِ مستوی

> His beauty intoxicating
> compelling us to gaze –
> yet I, my crude vision hampered,
> fail to see that He is.

In the hereafter it will be different. There we will all, as it
were, meet God. Provided of course, that we aspire sincerely for
such meeting and that our striving is equal to our aspiration. It

is this meeting of God and man for which man was created. The attraction we feel for beauty, for values, has been implanted in us for this very purpose. Our destiny cannot remain unfulfilled. We may achieve it in stages. But man must witness God eventually, in full manifestation of His eternal charm and beauty. The purpose of creation must triumph.

آدمی دید است باقی پوست است

دید آں باشد که دید دوست است

Man is a being with vision.
The sight of the Beloved is the only seeing.

The *eye* of the Holy Quran –

وَاعْلَمُوٓا اَنَّكُمْ مُّلَاقُوهُ

And know that you shall
certainly meet Him! (2:224)

– points to the same truth.
The Holy Prophet (on whom be peace and the blessings of God) has himself said something similar.

فَـيُرْفَعُ الْحِجَابُ فَيَنْظُرُوْنَ اِلٰى وَجْهِ اللّٰهِ فَمَا اُعْطُوْا شَيْئًا اَحَبَّ

اَلَيْهِمْ مِنَ النَّظَرِ اِلٰى رَبِّهِمْ ۔

The curtain will be raised and believers will see God in His Might and Glory. They will have their rewards but they will like no reward more than this meeting with their Lord (Mishkat).

We cannot see God in this world, in our present life. In this connection we should remember that knowledge comes by contrasts. If we had knowledge only of what day is like and had

never known what night is like, we would not have had full
knowledge of what day is like. We come to know what day is
because of what we know of night, the opposite of day. God is
unique in this respect. He has no opposite, no not-God. Everywhere we have God or signs of God, His light, His manifestation.
This then is the point. God has no contrast. He is evident and
everywhere. Because of this He cannot be seen. He lives in the
depths, in the recesses of all being. His beauty lies hidden, veiled.

کیا کھلے جو کبھی نہ تھا پنہاں

کیا ملے جو کبھی جدا نہ ہوا

> You found Him you think,
> Who never did hide?
> and met Him
> Who ever was by thy side?

In the Holy Quran we read about Moses asking to see God.
When God shows Himself in vision, Moses, unable to stand a
full view of God, becomes dazed, senseless. The narrative points
to the fact that the beauty of God is dazzling, humans cannot
stand it. A great prophet, Moses, sees God in a vision. He had
only a symbolic view. Even at this he drops down stunned,
senseless. Joseph's beauty is proverbial in our scriptures. How
he had charmed ladies of the court of Egypt! The knives they
were to use to cut the meat served before them, they struck on
their own hands. So stupefied were they at the sight of Joseph's
beauty! Didn't they cry aloud, 'He is no man, he is an angel'?

In short, beauty captivates. We cannot escape it. Thus earthly
beauty gives us some idea of beauty divine.

فکرم بمنتهائے جمالت نمی رسد

کز هر چه در خیالِ من آید نکوتری

Howsoever I may try
I can comprehend not
Thy Beauty Divine –
farther thou art
than the farthest I could imagine.

# XI

A doubt arises here which must be resolved. How can we be attracted to the beauty of God? God is without body and the physical eye cannot see Him. How do we get attracted and to what?

The answer is that Beauty is not confined to the physical. A well-proportioned body, rosy cheeks, youthful looks, freshness of face, are no doubt essential ingredients of beauty. But do we not talk of a beautiful city, a beautiful picture, a beautiful song or a beautiful character – all devoid of the commonly-known essentials of beauty. Yet we had beauty. What is beauty, then? Beauty is excellence, but excellence proper to the object, the beauty of which is in question, proper to the person whose beauty is being judged. When such excellence is present to a degree of perfection we call the person beautiful.

Now let us ponder. The perfections worthy of God, perfections attributable to the divine being, are all to be found in Him. Only He possesses the most perfect attributes, only He is free from defects, weaknesses. He is one and the only one. He has no equal, no partner. He is all-powerful. He is beneficent; that is, He confers and endows without any deserts. He gives without our asking or deserving. He is merciful. That is, He rewards our deeds fully. He is the Lord of all worlds. That is, He is the nourisher, the developer, the guarantor of progress. He raises the imperfect to perfection. Ultimate rewards and punishment are in His hands. Everything in this world, this universe, owes its existence and excellence to Him. He is unique, He is not begotten, but He creates everything. He is self-subsistent, but everything subsists because of Him. If He withdraws His sustaining hand, everything will come to naught. Death or decay or decline is not for Him. Everything without Him is subject to death and destruction. He is above want or need. But all things have wants and needs. He provides food and nourishment for

everyone, everything, but Himself is above the need of food or
drink. He is the supreme ruler. His rule is over everything, He
Himself is free from all limitations, all constraints. He is all-
hearing, all-seeing. Nothing is hidden from Him. Past, present
or future are the same for Him. No-one can interfere in His
plans, His wishes or wills. But not a leaf can move without His
will. He is above the limitations of time and space. He is the
originator, the source and spring of the entire universe. He is all-
wise, all-free in His actions and dealings, His power knows no
limits, His knowledge no gaps. His mercy encompasses everything. His forgiveness has precedence over His wrath. His
magnanimity knows no bounds, His mercy no limits. He forgives
without cause, without atonement. His mercy is all-embracing,
ultimate, basic. Yet He is master, mighty, and punishes when
He should. He would not treat loyal and disloyal servants alike.
If He did so, it would be a sign of weakness. He manifests
Himself with a new glory every day, every moment. The most
truly magnanimous is He. Others give in the hope of reward
hereafter, or to be praised here in this world. And they only give
out of what the Lord has given them. If the Lord had not given
*them*, they would have had nothing to give. They give out of what
the Lord has trusted them with. He provides for peace, protects
us from all afflictions, guards us against mishaps. He is dominant
over all, the One Who compensates us for our losses. He turns
to us with mercy ever and ever. His greatness is unique. He
shields us from the consequences of our mistakes, our sins. He
resolves for us our difficulties. Honour and disgrace are in His
hands, He is the One Who raises us in public esteem and pulls
us down if He so wills. He is the true judge and real justice
comes only from Him. His eye is on every small detail. His is
the true appreciation. Glory and greatness belong only to him.
He is the watcher of us all, the protector, the helper. He is the
One Who listens to the prayers of men, the One Who accepts
their prayers and their good deeds. He is most loving, most
worthy. His attributes are ever with Him. He is the most manifest, the most hidden, the very first, the very last. He is the
dispenser of forgiveness and He is the forgiver. Everything we
have is His gift. He is most tolerant, most patient, even with

those who are ungrateful or unmannerly. He is the One Who turns to men with mercy, and again and again. He is the possessor of all the good names. The Holy Prophet counted ninety-nine of them. But it would be wrong to think the ninety-nine names are the only names He has. This inadequate expression of His greatness and majesty is all that is possible for us earth-bound creatures of limited capacity and knowledge. His wonderful and glorious attributes surpass all description and understanding.

هَر چه آید بفهم و عقل و قیاس

ذاتِ او برتر است زان و سواس

Understanding and reasoning,
and imagining besides,
may do their utmost;
but beyond, ever beyond,
remains the core – the essence – of His Being.

Now you are the judge. A being, a person, of such attributes, who would say He is not entitled to our love and our worship? Shall we not give our full devotion, the devotion of our heart and soul to such a being? Is there another one deserving of our love in a like manner?

# XII

Another doubt may be disposed of here. That knowledge of all things does not come from seeing may be conceded. The beauty of music is appreciated by the ear, not the eye. But, it may be objected, even the ear is a source of sense-experience. How is the beauty of things appreciated which can be neither seen nor heard, nor smelt, nor touched? The answer is that beauty does not belong only to things known by sense-experience. There is such a thing as extra-sensory experience, the experience of moral qualities we perceive in others. We say so-and-so possesses admirable moral qualities or moral character. Does knowledge of moral qualities or moral character come from our five senses? Hardly. It comes rather from an inner sense. It is not sensory experience but rather moral experience we point to when we praise moral qualities or moral character. Good moral qualities or good moral character are welcome to everyone. Whoever possesses such qualities, such character is welcome. And naturally so.

Another interesting question arises here. It is said that love of God is embedded in the human heart like a seed sown in ground. Why was it sown as a seed and not made part and parcel of the nature of man like his other appetites and instincts? The answer is that where growth and development is the intention, there beginning is made with a seed. A seed has a potentiality, great potentiality. Appetites like hunger and thirst are compelling. This is because hunger and thirst are not destined to grow and develop. They are destined to remain as they are. Other human appetites and instincts are in the same class. Love of God is in a class by itself. It is meant to grow and develop and reach height after height. Therefore, love of God had to be implanted as a seed. It could then become a source of great possibilities and great progress.

There is another reason why love of God was implanted as a

seed. Natural dispositions must be left free if their exercise is to earn merit. Appetites and instincts are compelling, irresistible. Their exercise is not an act of merit. Merit comes of free activity. You can run a race in competition and win a prize. Appetites are not free. Their exercise deserves no reward.

# XIII

The second stimulus to love is beneficence or receiving graces without deserts. If someone treats you with graces you have not earned, you feel drawn to him. They say, 'Man is enslaved by grace.'

You see this natural response to grace even in wild animals. There is evidence in history on this point. Blood-sucking wild animals would show instant gratitude on recognizing their bene-factors. Men should do better. If men are found devoid of grati-tude in response to grace, are they men? No, they are beasts or even worse.

The graces – mercies and unearned benefits – we owe to God are countless, literally countless:

عنایت ہائے او را چوں شمارم
کہ لطفِ اوست بیروں از شمارے

His Graces, O His Graces!
how will I count?
Kindnesses galore –
beyond count are they.

Yet let us try and name and describe some of the more patent ones. Even this seems impossible. At once we begin to think of the many, many different kinds of graces we owe to our Lord.

The first thing to notice is that our very existence, our life and being, is entirely a gift of the gracious Lord. Had He not extended this privilege to us, we would not have found our way into this world of existence.

بادِ ما و بُودِ ما از دادِتُست

ہستئ ما جملہ از ایجادِتُست

What we were and what we are
we owe all to Thee.
Our existence, our being,
is designed and created –
all by Thee.

Let man think of his origin. There was a time when he was
nowhere. No sign of him anywhere. Then he appeared in the
form of a microscopic particle or worm. And this worm became
man.

کرمکے بُودم مرا کردی بشر

A tiny worm was I,
Thou madest me a man.

This growth from worm to man took place without any effort,
any solicitation on our part:

ما نہ بودیم وتقاضنہ ما نہ بود

لطفِ تو ناگفتہٗ ما می شنود

Existed we not
not asked we for aught –
Thou gavest all,
and Thou gavest of what
we knew nothing at all.

We came to exist and Thou didst provide for all we had need
of at the time.

تری عطا ہے میری احتیاج سے پہلے
کبھی سوال کی نوبت نہ تُونے آنے دی

Thy gifts come
sooner than I am able to ask –
Thou waitest not
for my prayers, my supplications.

After this passage of ours from nothing to something, we began to see more and ever more graces raining on us. To enumerate these is impossible. We lived, but completely unconscious, of everything, including ourselves. In a mother's womb we had everything provided for us. With utter kindness, out of sheer beneficence. This gives us an idea of what was done for us.

Then after birth – feeble and helpless in every way – we found our parents surrounding us with God-given tenderness, ready to do every little thing necessary to let us grow. Amazing all this, a jelly-like mass of flesh becomes the object of the tenderest attention on the part of a father and mother. They sacrifice their own comforts and devote themselves to the comfort of the infant and find their joy in it, their real unpretended joy. Who can say he had done something to deserve the unselfish, the completely disinterested services his parents rendered to him to bring him up? Then we come to live as one among the many, many denizens of this world. But already God our Creator has established a complicated but orderly complex of conditions under which we begin to live and grow. Most hospitable! And incredibly so! As if we were on the divine list of expected guests whose slightest needs had to be looked after! At birth we need the lightest possible nourishment. A mother's milk is ready to provide this. And yet another wonder, this mother's milk becomes heavier with time in consonance with a growing baby's digestive powers. The thin fluid that it was in the beginning becomes thicker and heavier. The baby needs it and can take it. The water part is now less, the food part more.

Just think of the Creator of this expansive, limitless universe, master, majestic, magnificent. To think of Him is to tremble in awe of Him. This Creator, what interest can He have in a tiny, helpless, albeit living creature? Yet look at the magnanimity with which He deals with him. Sooner than his arrival are assembled all the provisions, the conditions necessary for his life, health and growth. And not just assembled. There is awareness among these provisions that they must change with change in the needs of the baby.

For the maintenance of life what appropriate organs and powers have been endowed – eyes to see, ears to hear, a tongue to judge how things taste, a nose to judge smells, hands to work with, also, legs to move about with, a brain to do all the imagining, thinking, and concentrating. These powers are gifts great, given freely to us by our Creator. And yet so neglectful are we, hardly ever do we think what marvellous gifts are these. But now and then we do think. That is when for some cause – maybe illness or accident – we temporarily lose the use of any one of these powers, these organs. The power to ambulate, for instance. How many of us and how often do we think of it and thank God for it? But ask someone who knows, some unfortunate one who has lost the use of an eye or ear or limb.

اے خُدا احسانِ تو اندر شمار        می نتانم بر زبانِ صد ہزار

جان و گوش و چشم و ہوش و پاؤ دست        جملہ از دُر ہائے احسانت پُر است

Countless Thy favours,
O God!
A hundred thousand tongues
can deliver not the thanks
due to Thee:
my life, my eyes, my ears,
my hands, my feet,
my consciousness all, are
proof of Thy beneficence,
Thy concern, Thy graces.

Think that we have someone who lives in a distant land and

who has sent an army of servants for our use. These servants
are busy day and night serving us in all sorts of ways. They ask
for no wages, and we have no means for making the least bit of
return for these unpaid services. What should be our feelings for
such a donor or benefactor? Remember that all our powers, our
senses, our limbs are those unpaid servants of ours, whom the
Creator has appointed to serve us round the clock.

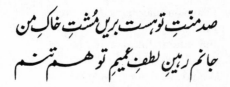

Favours upon favours
hast Thou showered
on this handful of dust:
life entire
is indebted to Thee,
Thy universal care.

Our benevolent Creator – oh, how He takes charge of us and
provides for all our needs after our birth! To think of this is to
go into ecstasy. There is the sun at 90,000,000 miles from our
earth, the light and heat of which makes our life on this earth
possible. The earth rotates round its axis and makes day and
night alternate for us. The earth also revolves round the sun,
once every year and makes our four seasons. The sun, the seas,
the winds that blow over them, the mountains, one and all
contribute to maintaining our earth in life and lustre. Winds
laden with water distilled from the bitter salt, the water of the
oceans, blow over us and bring us rainwater to drink and to feed
our crops. They cross the thousands and thousands of miles –
over ocean and ocean – only to come and serve us. How much
does it cost to fetch a pail of water from the nearest well or tap?
From this calculate the cash value of water that rains on us every
year. The figures will be staggering. The poet Sadi said well on
the subject:

ابرو باد و مہ و خورشید و فلک درکارند    تا تو نانے بکف آری و بغفلت نخوری

ہمہ از بہر تو سرگشتہ و فرماں بردار    شرط انصاف نباشد کہ تو فرماں نبری

> The clouds, the winds,
> the moon, sun and sky,
> busy with their appointed tasks –
> why?
> That you may have your bread
> and eat,
> and ungrateful need not be,
> and all these are for Thee.
> Would it be fair
> if thou obeyest not Him
> Who does all for thee?

Uncounted varieties of minerals buried underground serve us in a thousand different ways. Modern industrial civilization, and man's sway over nature, which, after conquering the winds and the waves, culminated in a landing on the moon, would have been impossible without this buried wealth. And because the land area of the globe is only a third of the area under water the treasures which await discovery on the ocean bed far surpass the treasures buried in the continents. On the basis of the area the treasures under the seas should be thrice as much, but in fact they are much more abundant. And their variety is endless. The astonishing success of the modern machine age in its fight against poverty would have been impossible without these buried treasures. The western people who worship material progress with inordinate pride should ponder whether they would have achieved their high living standards if the earth had been devoid of these hidden treasures. And they should ask of themselves as to who created the intellect which bore such wonderful fruit?

Let man look at his daily food. What different things are there that he can eat? Of different kinds, different tastes. Things to eat, things to drink, so many that we hardly need them all. Plenty and variety are both there. We owe it all to the wide, liberal and universal beneficence of our Creator. On our table are spread so many things to eat, and of so many kinds. Cereals of all kinds, vegetables, roots, meats, fruits of many different colours and typical of their seasons. Then there are the milch animals. And what a miracle of taste and nourishment is milk! There are the honey-bees which collect honey for us from flowers. There are things, in short, in incredible abundance and variety, to please our palate and to fill our stomachs, which our Creator has provided for us. All out of His grace, His beneficence. To contemplate all this is to bow in gratitude.

And let us not forget our clothing, the things we wear or use as drapery for our bodies. We may use cotton or wool or (as now) many another fibre. Out of these are made clothes for use in summer and winter. They are light and soft and warm and serve us in climates hot and cold. And the silk-worm which spins out a shiny, soft yarn, that we may make manifold the already rich variety of fabrics we have for everyday use. We have synthetic fibres now. And these have ushered in a revolution in human apparel. Has not our Creator shown to us His magnanimity in the matter of clothing, as He has in the matter of food? Chemical fertilizers have multiplied the food-wealth we could raise from our land. Chemical fibres are doing the same for our clothing. In short, our Creator has provided and He keeps providing for our increasing population and a wonderful provision it is.

آں کہ بدہد بے امیدے سُود ہا

آں خُدا است و خُدا است و خُدا

He Who gives generously
and gives for no return –
He is God, He is God, He is God.

# XIV

If the question is raised about the poverty and want which stalk many parts of the world, condemning vast sections of the human population to go unclad, unfed, the answer is, whose fault? There is no lack of magnanimity on the part of our Creator. The lack is of knowledge and its application. If a Pakistani peasant or a peasant from some other backward country is unable to raise as much yield out of 1 acre as can a peasant from Japan, then who is to blame? Students of economics know too well how much the human factor – human knowledge and human effort and skill – has to do with making a country or a people rich or poor. Our Creator has endowed the earth with inexhaustible sources of economic wealth. How much wealth a given part of the earth yields will depend on the hard work, the skill and knowledge applied by man. The best part of a country's wealth is its manpower, both quantity and quality. The capacities and character of the population play a crucial part. It is these we must take care of, if we want a country to progress. Our Creator is magnanimous beyond measure. It is the people, the men and women who inhabit a land, who have to put their God-given capacities to use. If they do this well, they can turn the fortunes of their country. Japan has set the example. Japan has very little of its own resources in material wealth, yet it stands in the front rank of advanced countries today. All this has happened in the last hundred years. The way standards of living have shot up in Japan is an eye-opener for all backward parts of the world.

Food and clothing are the basic needs of man. But shelter – a roof to live under – is no less basic. And what has our Creator not provided for it? Earth, wood, iron, stone, marble, glass are provided just for this purpose. That we may have strong, secure and comfortable houses to live in. People in the more developed countries have put to use these God-given resources and built beautiful houses for themselves. The residential areas of their towns seem like paradise upon earth. Those who travel to these countries and see what man has created for himself can easily see that this would have been impossible had not our Creator created the materials needed for house-building.

The abilities with which human beings happen to be endowed – different in different individuals – are a tremendous gift of God to man. Differences in these abilities which different individuals display are also a gift and a boon. To run the world and do the many different kinds of things which must be done, different kinds of abilities are required. If all men had the same abilities, each in the same degree, how could our world have functioned?

# XV

What we have so far said of the mercy, magnanimity and beneficence of God is evident enough. Everybody can see it in his own person and in the facts of the world spread out before him. Still, the fact remains that what meets the eye is insignificant compared with what one perceives when one begins to go deep and see below the surface or behind the curtain, as it were. In this essay of modest dimensions we cannot go into any great details. Only hints of what modern science has to teach may be possible.

And these would be enough to show that anything we try to study in some depth only reveals the unlimited grace and bounty of God-grace and bounty meant only to promote our life, our purposes.

How does our gracious God manage to maintain our life on this earth? Let us have a brief glance at this. This is what we find. Our earth is a round ball suspended in space, in constant motion – called rotation – round its own axis. This rotation gives us the alternation of day and night, so that we work during the day and rest during the night. Besides rotating thus our earth also revolves round the sun and completes each revolution once every year. These movements keep the earth steady in the same direction. At the same time, the axis round which the earth moves is not erect but inclined at an angle of approximately 23 degrees. This incline yields us our four seasons (every schoolboy knows about it). The earth's surface-spherical surface – is enveloped round to a height of about 500 miles by gases of all kinds. These are essential to our continued life on the surface of the earth. A thick layer of this girdling envelope also protects us from those meteorites which keep raining on us from outer space. About 20 million of them, travelling at 30 miles per second, keep piercing the gaseous envelope. Besides performing its other functions, this envelope also keeps our temperatures within limits. (The limits are essential to our continued life.) The present

size of our earth is just the right size for it. It could have been
neither larger nor smaller than it is. For instance, if it had been
no larger than the moon, its force of gravity would have been
reduced to one-sixth of its present force. This would have resulted
in the evaporation of air and water. Were the earth twice its
present size, its force of gravity would have doubled, the envelope
of air would have lost its present shape, making our life on earth
impossible. About the distance of the earth from the sun, had it
been twice as long, the heat we receive from the sun would have
been reduced to one-quarter, which also would have made life
impossible. On the other hand, if the distance of the earth had
been reduced to one-half, the heat of the sun would have in-
creased to four times its present heat; again life would have
become impossible. In short, the present size of our earth, its
present rates of rotation and revolution, the inclination of its axis
of rotation at a certain angle, its present distance from the sun,
its girdle of life-supporting gases – all these (and many other
things which we don't know about) are arrangements designed
by our gracious Lord and Creator, to make our life on earth both
possible and pleasant. Pleasant in a thousand and one different
ways. The Holy Quran has something to say on this very point:

وَإِنْ تَعُدُّوا نِعْمَةَ اللهِ لَا تُحْصُوهَا

And He gave you all that you wanted of Him; and if you try
to count the favours of Allah, you will not be able to number
them. Verily, man is very unjust, very ungrateful (14:35).

## XVI

These graces of our Lord are not limited to our physical and physiological needs. We have the thought expressed most beautifully in –

آنکه بر تن کرد این لطفِ اتم
کے کند محروم جاں را از کرم

> He Who has endowed the body
> with favours great –
> will He deny the soul
> graces equally great?

He Who bestowed such favours on our body could not treat our souls with lesser concern. He gave us the gift of reason so that we could recognize Him, and then, by decreeing that communion with Him would be the goal of our existence, opened to us avenues of unending spiritual progress. Just as His grace and splendour are infinite, so also our spiritual journey in His quest must be endless and ever onwards. If His beauties had been limited, man, in their contemplation, would eventually have become satiated; and that which satiates ceases to attract. But in the contemplation of Divine attributes there is neither any limit nor any satiation. This is the reason for man's eternal life in the hereafter. The desire to live for ever is planted deep in man's being; and to plant a desire, and not to provide for its satisfaction would have been unworthy of His mercy and beneficence. That is why He has decreed that the human soul once created would not be destroyed:

جوہرِ انساں عدم سے ناآشنا ہوتا نہیں

آنکھ سے غائب تو ہوتا ہے فنا ہوتا نہیں

The soul of man
is not fated to disappear – it
goes out of sight –
into nothingness it does not fade.

The death of our earthly body is not our extinction. It is but a shift to a more exalted existence, with far greater possibilities for communion with the divine being than are possible in this mundane life. The ultimate glory of life is a vision of the supreme being, and the path to that vision lies in the shedding of ephemeral attachments and entanglements:

کمالِ زندگی دیدارِ ذات است

طریقش رُستن از بندِ جہات است

Life's destiny is vision,
vision of God:
the way to it is freedom,
freedom from space, and
freedom from time.

Compared to the hereafter, our worldly life is like existence in our mother's dark and small womb. If we had been told before our birth, that after a brief sojourn in the womb, we would arrive in a vast universe with possibilities of unlimited progress, the idea would have been incomprehensible. But it would have been true. In the same way, death cannot mean annihilation. Our beneficent Creator, for this short, earthly life, bestows unlimited resources on us, and nurtures us in a thousand wondrous ways. That He should then Himself send us into dark extinction like a snuffed-out candle is inconceivable. That would be unworthy of

the great Creator, who with infinite mercy sustains us through
stage after stage of our growth.

ہے مَوت میں ضرور کوئی راز دل نشیں سب کچھ کے بعد کچھ بھی نہیں، یہ تو کچھ نہیں

Death must have
some meaning deep –
for, if dissolution be the end,
with nothing after it,
then all this is nothing, just nothing at all.

To do so would be contrary to His eternal wisdom; for we can
witness all around us His sublime universal law of the evolutionary growth of the inferior to the superior. This yearning
towards Him is manifested by every particle, whether at rest or
in motion.

جملہ اجزا در تحرک در سکوں

ناطق ان انَّا اِلَیۡهِ رَاجِعُوۡن

All things moving,
all things still,
proclaim – 'we are destined
only for Him.'

Let man study himself. At one stage he was no more than the
elements from which he was subsequently formed. Could his
progress to becoming a human being have been possible without
the working of the beneficent law of evolution. The Almighty is
not only the Creator, He is also the sustainer, who continues to
give life ever better opportunities of progress and development.
From the dawn of creation until the present times, man has
passed through many different stages, and each stage has been
better than the preceding one. Unlimited progress would have
been impossible without this evolutionary sequence of death and

extinction in one form, and rebirth and appearance in a better one. Let us look at our food. We eat the products of vegetables, minerals, etc. which are broken down and digested only to reappear as parts of our bodies. Our food is the basis of our lives. Without food neither could our bodies exist, nor could we remain rational creatures endowed with intellect and reason. It would therefore be no exaggeration to say that intellect and reason are only a manifestation of our food in a higher form. And all of history bears witness that intellect itself performs wonders and miracles in the course of its own evolutionary progress. Everything in the universe is subject to the profoundly sagacious law of evolution. To this law man is no exception. And this law is inviolable. Our bodily death is also subject to it. Therefore, for anything in continuous growth and progress, every new stage must be better and higher than every earlier stage. Each new stage comes into being out of nothing and provides clear and conclusive proof that the Almighty is the supreme Creator and the compassionate sustainer.

هے ايو وليوشن بس اک تفسير ربّ العالمين
کاش اس نقطے سے واقف ہوں مسلمان ان دنوں

The exegesis of the Nourisher of the world
is evolution.
Would that Muslims learned this meaning.

# XVII

The ultimate reality of life after death must remain a mystery in this existence, but the stage of dreaming provides a pointer. Our bodily senses become inactive during sleep and cease to function; but that does not apply to the soul, which is the epitome of a man's individuality. Without utilizing any of our physical organs the soul continues to function normally during dreaming. Without using the physical eyes or the physical ears, or the physical tongue, or the physical limbs, it can see, and can hear, and can taste, and can move about exactly as when awake. The limitations of space and time vanish. The impossible becomes easy and simple. We soar like a bird, and move instantly from one end of the earth to the other. We travel a thousand miles in the twinkling of an eye; and meet persons long since dead. And the dream has the conviction of reality; so that as we awaken from a nightmare in sweaty terror we breathe a sigh of relief. The beauty and peace of a pleasant dream linger on long afterwards. Our physical eyes and other parts of our bodies neither function nor participate in it, yet the dream is remembered with clarity.

How is it that though our eyes did not see it, yet we saw something of which we retain full recollection?

The answer is that it was seen by our soul. The soul has its independent existence even though God has also linked it to our material body. The soul has a world of its own, in which it is free of the limitations which apply to the time and space of our material body and its organs. When the material body dies, the soul continues to exist in its own world. The world of dream is a pointer to the potential hidden within our souls.

The devotees of worldly wisdom who deny the existence of the soul may ridicule this idea. To them nothing non-material, such as a soul, is possible, and there can be no link between the body and anything non-material. But, surely, they cannot deny the existence of the intellect: intellect itself is a non-material entity, and no-one can deny its link to the human brain. There is an inherent contradiction in the philosopher's denial of a link between the body and the soul. It is like the denial of someone answering a knock at his door by saying 'I am not in.'

The western psychologists' view of the soul is very much like this denial. And yet in their experiments in psychoanalysis, they have uncovered a whole range of phenomena which they ascribe to the human subconscious. A little reflection shows that the psychoanalysts' subconscious and the soul are two names for the same reality. Psychologists' experiments reveal that under hypnotic sleep a person can recall in detail all those events in his life which had been forgotten by his conscious mind. This recall is possible, because the memory of his past actions is retained permanently within the subconscious; and because the subconscious is free from all limitations of space and time.

Psychologists' experiments prove the existence in this life of a human faculty which is free of the limitations of time and space. As this is also the essence of the soul, what is the point in differentiating between them?

The world of dreams provides a clear understanding of the existence of the soul. The soul has an independent existence; is free of the limitations of time and space; and can function with or without its links with our material bodies. Death cannot destroy the soul. Death only sets it free from the human body.

## XVIII

In short, questions usually raised between religious believers and others – what happens after death? what may be meant by resurrection, the judgment day, heaven, hell, and so on – are questions about which certain knowledge cannot be had. Not like the knowledge we can have of things of this world, things we study in natural and social sciences. The reason is obvious. Human knowledge cannot rise above the level of development which human personality can attain in this life. While we belong to this world, we cannot understand the nature of the next. Descriptions of the hereafter, therefore, fall back upon symbols and metaphors and experiences derived from life here. The joys of paradise, for instance, will have to be described in terms of joys we know here. The Holy Quran and Hadith use just this method for the elucidation of life hereafter. There is no other way open. Unfortunately not only common people, but even scholars – who ought to know better – have taken the scriptural descriptions in their literal sense. Yet if they had but read their scripture with some little care, they would have found that this is not the correct approach to an understanding of the scriptural descriptions. The scriptural descriptions are metaphorical, this being the only way open to bring home their meaning to us. Says God in the Holy Quran:

مَثَلُ الْجَنَّةِ الَّتِيْ وُعِدَ الْمُتَّقُوْنَ ۔

That is, the description of paradise is a metaphorical not a literalist description (47:16).

فَلَا تَعْلَمُ نَفْسٌ مَّآ اُخْفِيَ لَهُمْ مِّنْ قُرَّةِ اَعْيُنٍ ۔

And no souls know what joy of the eyes is kept hidden for them, as a reward for their good works (32:18).

The joys of paradise are not reproductions of the joys of this world but only their images. Were it not so, the joys of paradise would not have been described as joys kept hidden from the believers. 'Milk', 'pomegranates', 'grapes', 'honey', we know and use. They are not secrets hidden from us. Used for paradise they must be understood as images or metaphors. Again the Holy Prophet himself has said about paradise:

$$\text{لَا عَيْنَ رَأَتْ وَلَا أُذُنَّ سَمِعَتْ وَلَا خَطَرَ عَلَى قَلْبِ بَشَرٍ ـ}$$

No eye hath seen it, no ear hath heard it, no man hath any conception of it.

The Word of God and the words of the Holy Prophet both hold the joys of paradise as new and unique, unknown, except for their resemblance in spirit with the joys of this world. We cannot think of the former as literal continuations of the latter. If we do, we should be moving away from the spirit of the scriptural teaching. 'Day of judgment', 'resurrection', 'the great balance', 'paradise', 'hell' are all valid and true, but they are not to be taken literally. They are appropriate metaphors and similes for what we have yet to know. It is their essence or hidden meaning we must take, not their outer superficial sense. That would be wrong, utterly wrong. It would be naive and childish in the extreme to think of God as a monarch of the fables, sitting on a huge throne, the dead rising out of their graves, accounts of their past deeds in their hands, appearing before Him, and ordered to paradise or to hell, as the case may be, and all this happening in a vast, fearful gathering. Is it thus we should think of the deity? In outright, primitive physical terms? God save us from such thought! No, no, God is holy, free from physical blemishes. Descriptions of the hereafter to be found in the Holy Quran are all valid. But they must be understood in terms consistent with the central image of the God of the Quran – holy, pure spirit, transcendent, possessor of the most perfect attributes. There must be no contradiction between the essence of these descriptions and the naive images and pictures which they arouse in our minds.

What happens at death? Only the soul leaves the bodily frame which has served it until now, as a shell, a holder or a base. When body and soul part with each other, death is only for the body, not for the soul. And why? Because we are destined by our Creator to go from here to an hereafter, a new world of possibilities and unheard-of progress. In this new world our crude present physical frame is unable to function. But the soul will yet have a body; body of a new sort. The spirit of every thing needs a shell, a container, the function of which is only to hold it. This new frame will grow out of our deeds in this world. Good deeds will lend us a spiritual body, capable of viewing God, Who is Himself Spirit. Those who take good deeds with them from here will view God hereafter and will be in the Garden with Him. But black deeds will lend us a black body. Dark itself, it will be unable to view God Who is pure light. Darkness cannot be reconciled with light. They are poles apart. No wonder, therefore, sinners will be deprived of a vision of God, until, of course, they are reclaimed.

Thus of the inmates of paradise we have the Holy Quran tell us this:

يَوۡمَ تَرَى الۡمُؤۡمِنِيۡنَ وَالۡمُؤۡمِنٰتِ يَسۡعٰى نُوۡرُهُمۡ بَيۡنَ اَيۡدِيۡهِمۡ وَ بِاَيۡمَانِهِمۡ ۔

And *think* of the day when thou wilt see the believing men and the believing women, their light running before them and on their right hands, *and will be said to them*, 'Glad tidings for you this day.' Gardens through which streams flow, wherein you will abide. That is the supreme triumph (57:13).

And again:

وَالَّذِيۡنَ اٰمَنُوۡا مَعَهٗ نُوۡرُهُمۡ يَسۡعٰى بَيۡنَ اَيۡدِيۡهِمۡ وَبِاَيۡمَانِهِمۡ يَقُوۡلُوۡنَ رَبَّنَاۤ اَتۡمِمۡ لَنَا نُوۡرَنَا وَاغۡفِرۡ لَنَاۤ اِنَّكَ عَلٰى كُلِّ شَىۡءٍ قَدِيۡرٌ ۔

Their light will run before them and on their right hands.

They will say, 'Our Lord perfect our light for us and forgive us; surely Thou hast power over all things' (66:9).

The inmates of paradise keep praying to God, for more and yet more light. What does it show? That spiritual progress here-after will be unending. There will be after each achievement a still higher achievement. Finding one they will implore for another still more perfect. After this, one still more perfect and so on. Knowledge of God will be unending. There will always be something new and more to aspire for and to achieve:

ہر لحظہ نیا طُور نئی برقِ تجلّی
اللہ کرے مرحلۂ شوق نہ ہو طے

Every moment comes to view,
a new Sinai, a new lighting!
I wish to God
it would go on like this,
This eternal longing, this quest.

This is what we call infinite beauty. It is beauty of God. Its vision is ever-beckoning, ever-exciting.

Of the inmates of hell, God said:

وَ مَنْ كَانَ فِيْ هٰذِهٖ أَعْمٰى فَهُوَ فِى الْأَخِرَةِ أَعْمٰى وَأَضَلُّ سَبِيْلًا

But who is blind in this world will be blind in the Hereafter, and even more astray from the way (17:73).

The verse is an eye-opener. Will you take it literally? Then it will make no sense. A man blinded for some reason in the world here, will rise blind in the hereafter? Physically, that is to say? No.

What the verse means is that a good life lived here sharpens the believer's vision for knowledge of God hereafter. So a bad life dulls the sinner's vision for such knowledge hereafter. The sinner remains spiritually blind, deprived and distanced. Reward and punishment, which we meet with hereafter, do not come from outside. They grow naturally from our own deeds and are the natural consequences of those deeds. What we do here is presented to us hereafter as the consequence – only more concrete – of what we do here. Punishment hereafter is not arbitrary, the pleasure of the divine despot, but the consequence in the concrete of our own bad deeds. The sinner will recognize it as his own doing. Similarly rewards hereafter – the joys of paradise – are a consequence of the doer's good deeds.

About hell, let us remember the divine promise.

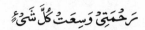

My Mercy encompasseth all things (7:157).

According to this, even hell is proof of divine mercy. Does not the sick man who knows what he should do make for a hospital, where arrangements exist for restoring him to health? He suffers all the pains involved and even spends and gives for their sake and for the sake of the health that results from them. He even submits to surgery. Why? Only that he may have health again. This is exactly what our gracious Lord and Creator will do for those who go spiritually sick from here, so that the impediments to the spiritual destiny – the end of our being – which they themselves had created may disappear. It was the destiny they had missed by their own deeds. It is what they will now reach. Hell is not a place for punitive exercise. It is a place for re-education, reform. It is wrong to think of divine rewards and punishments as arbitrary findings delivered to suit the whims of the divine despot. Many anti-religionists think so. The Holy Quran describes hell as the sinner's 'mother'.

أُمُّهُ هَاوِيَةٌ

Their mother is Hell (101:10).

A child is carried by a mother in her womb only for such time

as is necessary. Necessary for the requirements of life after birth.
The mother is all affection, all concern for the child. The meta-
phor is full of meaning: where there is love, there is also punishment, but punishment not for the pleasure of it but for the good
of the child. Hell is a reformatory; its purpose is reform, re-
education, recovery. Hell, therefore, is not – it cannot be – a
permanent institution. True, there are expressions in the Holy
Book which may be so construed (misconstrued to be exact).
*Khalidina fi ha abada* ('will live there for ever') only means a good
length of time. We have decisive passages in the Holy Quran on
this subject. Inmates of paradise and inmates of hell are
described, as it were, in parallel columns:

فَاَمَّاالَّذِيْنَ شَقُوْافَفِى النَّارِ لَهُمْ فِيْهَا زَفِيْرٌ وَّشَهِيْقٌ ه خَالِدِيْنَ

فِيْهَا مَا دَامَتِ السَّمٰوٰتُ وَالْاَرْضُ اِلَّا مَا شَآءَ رَبُّكَ اِنَّ رَبَّكَ فَعَّالٌ

لِّمَا يُرِيْدُ ه وَاَمَّاالَّذِيْنَ سُعِدُوْافَفِى الْجَنَّةِ خٰلِدِيْنَ فِيْهَامَادَامَتِ

السَّمٰوٰتُ وَالْاَرْضُ اِلَّا مَا شَآءَ رَبُّكَ عَطَآءً غَيْرَ مَجْذُوْذٍ ه

As for those who will prove unfortunate, they shall be in the
Fire, wherein there shall be for them sighing and sobbing.

Abiding therein so long as the heavens and the earth endure,
excepting what thy Lord may will. Surely, thy Lord brings
about what He pleases.

But as for those who will prove fortunate they shall be in
Heaven, abiding therein so long as the heavens and the earth
endure, excepting what thy Lord may will – a gift that shall
never be cut off (11:107–9).

If hell were a permanent institution, as indeed is paradise,
why not the same expression to project permanence of both? The
rewards of paradise are clearly described as rewards 'which will
cease not', unambiguously and eloquently permanent. But this

is not said of the punishments of hell. Why not? The Quran
passage is loud about one permanence, silent about the other.
And yet it is one and the same passage which describes both
paradise and hell. What does it mean? Only this, that hell is a
temporary institution, to serve for a term.

The Holy Prophet's own declaration is decisive:

$$\text{يَاْتِى عَلٰى جَهَنَّمَ زَمَانٌ لَيْسَ فِيْهَا اَحَدٌ ـ}$$

A time will come on hell when it will be empty of all inmates
(Maalamal-Tauzil).

# XIX

It may be said that we have presented only one side of the medal. What about the pain and anguish, the fatalities, the destruction that are the misfortune of man? Our reply is that what comes from the Creator carries wisdom in it. The wisdom is hidden. It may not show at once. We have seers like Akbar Allahabadi who have spotted this:

غم میں بھی قانونِ فطرت سے میں کچھ بدظن نہیں

یہ سمجھتا ہوں کہ میرا دوست ہے دُشمن نہیں

> Not even in grief
> do I cease to trust
> the law of Nature:
> for, I take it as a friend
> not a foe.

For instance, of all the ills that can befall man on earth the most terrifying is his own death, his destruction. But death – as we have already said – is an essential condition, a necessary means of man's own progress. Besides, the march of progress requires that generations of individuals should die and new generations take their place. Only thus can continuous progress be assured. Also, if death could be eliminated, the unchecked increase in the world's population will mean that pretty soon there will not be enough room for everyone to live. Earth will itself become hell for those who object to death as a rule of existence. They will themselves begin to ask for it. Who does not know what social scientists and economists keep saying? They are all for a moderate birthrate balanced by a natural death-rate.

We must not also forget that the wisdom of the divine order may not be apparent at once. But, when it does reveal itself, it fills man with a sense of wonder – a sense of true miraculous design. Our own failure to spot divine wisdom in God's designs is no proof that wisdom does not exist. The primitive man for example altogether failed to discover any wisdom in uranite (mineral of uranium). But with advance in knowledge we have discovered a new source of boundless energy hidden in this apparently dead mass of matter.

Further we must remember that misfortunes and miseries come to rouse unsuspected powers in man. What is called achievement and progress is nothing but dealing successfully with difficult situations:

تندئ ئ بادِ مخالف سے نہ گھبرا اے عقاب
یہ تو چلتی ہے تجھے اُونچا اُڑانے کے لیے

Fear not, O eagle!
the fierce wind that blows
from in front of thee:
'tis to help thee fly,
higher than high.

The second thing to remember is that if there were no pain or anguish in the world, there would be no happiness, no peace either.

رنج و غم را حق پئے آں آفرید
تا بدیں ضد خوش دلی آید پدید

Pain and anguish
did God create –
that we may enjoy life
by contrast.

The third thing to remember is that trials are trials. They bring no joy to God. Nor any knowledge God does not already have of the internal states of men. They reveal – to men – their capabilities, their potentialities. They provide a diagnosis, a measure of men's pace in their march to progress:

آں خدا را میرسد کو امتحاں       پیش آرد ہر دمے با بندگاں

تا بما ما را نمــاید آشکار       کہ چہ داریم از عقیدہ درسرار

> It is God's Right –
> He should put us to test
> every now and then
> that we come to know
> what we are at heart.

If there were no trials, there will be no knowing how and where we stand.

Also, how shall we acquire the power to endure, except if we confront difficulties and dangers? How does gold become free of dross unless it is allowed to melt in a crucible?

Evil – and evil is of many kinds – is also picked on as something contrary to divine mercy. But pause a little. Take anything 'evil' by itself. In itself you will find nothing evil in it. Fire burns and kills and destroys, true. But fire does other things, all merciful. Fire promotes civilization, runs industries. There would have been none of these, if we did not have fire. Fire is not evil. It is good. It is the evil *use* of it that makes it evil. Evil use of a thing meant for good use is disobedience of the Creator. War, violence, murder, arson and marauding are evil, but they are acts of disobedience of the Creator. They are acts forbidden. Would you ask why there is no fire which is incapable of being put to bad *use*? The answer to this is, it is illogical, asking for the impossible. Could fire burn and cool at the same time? Could it perform the functions both of fire and water? Could a thing serve as poison and antidote at the same time?

If it could, it would be to put two contradictories together, which is impossible.

In short, there is no such thing as evil as such. Every so-called evil has good in it. It is the use we make of things which makes them evil.

A study of how our universe has been created shows the sagacious wisdom of the Almighty Lord. By setting us challenging goals he has provided unlimited scope for our growth and progress. It would have been futile to have made this life a paradise where there were only comforts and pleasures; for moral values can have meanings only in a world where a choice exists between good and evil. It is a virtue to do good to someone, and a sin to do evil to someone; but neither would be possible, if, as in paradise, no-one needed any help and no-one feared any injury. Where good and evil are equally unpractical no opportunity can exist for moral or ethical action.

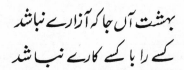

The Garden hereafter knows no pain, no problems, no dependence of one upon another.

Paradise is without suffering and without possibility of anyone being injured. For the formation and development of moral and ethical values, we need a world such as ours, where evil co-exists with good. It is a pity that this self-evident truth is not appreciated by those with a superficial approach. A school or a gymnasium is essential for our mental and physical development; for similar reasons this world is the appropriate place for the development of our moral and spiritual faculties. And just as a school is only for a brief sojourn, so is this world only a temporary abode. Those who grieve at the impermanent and transitory nature of life should realize that our mortality is in fact one of the Creator's greatest favours to us. We owe gratitude to our Creator for making it so. True, we have grief, and now and then suffer bereavement. Grief and sorrow help to build man's moral character. Listen to the poet:

دیدهٔ بینا میں داغِ غم چراغِ سینہ ہے

رُوح کو سامانِ زینت آہ کا آئینہ ہے

حادثاتِ غم سے ہے انساں کی فطرت کو کمال

غازہ ہے آئینۂ دل کے لیے گردِ ملال

طائرِ دل کے لیے غم شہپر پرواز ہے

راز ہے انساں کا دل غم انکشافِ راز ہے

غم نہیں غم رُوح کا اِک نغمۂ خاموش ہے

جو سرودِ بربطِ ہستی سے ہم آغوش ہے

شام جس کی آشنائے نالۂ "یا رب" نہیں

جلوہ پیرا جس کی شب میں اشک کے کوکب نہیں

جس کا جامِ دل شکستِ غم سے ہے نا آشنا

جو سدا مستِ شرابِ عیش و عشرت ہی رہا

ہاتھ جس گلچیں کا ہے محفوظ نوکِ خار سے

عشق جس کا بے خبر ہے ہجر کے آزار سے

کلفتِ غم گرچہ اس کے روز و شب سے دُور ہے

زندگی کا راز اس کی آنکھ سے مستُور ہے

Grief's darkness
for a discerning eye
is like a lamp
for the anguished heart.
Sobs and sighs
only animate the soul.

This God-given nature
achieves its perfection
through experiences of grief:
the dust of pain –
a polish for the mirror
of man's heart.

If the heart be a bird
then grief is its mighty wing!
The heart is a mystery
grief is the key,
its unlocking.

Grief is not grief,
'tis the song the soul sings
to resonate in silence,
with nature's own strings.

Who at sundown
has raised not his hands
to say 'O my Lord?'
Who has never let tears drop down
to join him in the stillness
of the night?
Whose brimful heart
has suffered not
the slightest touch of grief or pain?
Who has enjoyed
uninterruptedly
the pleasures of this life?

Flowers who has plucked
without a single thorny prick?
Who has loved but never known
the pain of separation from his love?

Is there such a man,
who truly knows
neither pain, nor grief?
Then knows he not
the mysteries of life.

And listen now to Maulana Rumi. How beautifully does he
counsel:

بنده می نالد بحق از دردِ خویش      صد شکایت می کند از رنجِ نیش

حق همی گوید که آخر رنج و درد      مر ترا لا به کناں ورا است کرد

این گله زاں نعمتے کن کمت زند

از درِ ما دور و مطرودت کند

در حقیقت هر عدو و داروئی تست      کیمیائے نافع و دل جوئی تست

که از و اندر گریزی در حــلا      استعانت جوئی از فضلِ خُدا

در حقیقت دوستانت دُشمنند

که ز حضرت دُور و مشغولت کنند

Lamenting a man entered
the presence of the Lord
to complain of a hundred or more
stings of pain.

Said God in reply:
'Your anguish has only humbled you
and made you pray
to become righteous again.

'Lament instead the many favours
bestowed upon you,
which kept you away from our Door.
Every enemy, if you really know,
is a potion, an antidote
for your moral lapses,
a well-wisher he comes to console.

'Does he not send you
to a cloister
where – alone – in the Great Presence
you ask for God's Mercy and Grace?

'Who are your enemies
your friends who take you away
from His presence,
and make you indifferent and negligent
towards Him?'

And how much pain and misery and suffering do men create
for the world? We have Hitler's example before us.

But it may be objected, why was man allowed to have so much
power to put to such bad use? The answer is, why is man given
the freedom to use or abuse his powers? Freedom is freedom to
do good or evil. If man were not free but constrained, and
constrained to do only good, he would have ceased to be man
and become instead an angel. Angels have no freedom. Angels
have to carry out the tasks for which they are commissioned. But
man was made for progress, for achievement, for going forward.
He had to have the freedom to move and move in any direction
he should choose. He should have been free to go forward or
backward, go right or go wrong. Now, if a man, instead of going

forward, chooses to go backward, who is to blame except himself? The Holy Quran expresses the point pithily:

لَقَدْ خَلَقْنَا الْإِنسَانَ فِى اَحْسَنِ تَقْوِيمٍ ه ثُمَّ رَدَدْنَاهُ اَسْفَلَ سَفِلِينَ ه

Indeed we created man in the fairest of all forms: but We let him degrade himself to the lowest of the low (95:8–9).

# XX

The third source or motive of love is perfection; it may be in any field, any direction. A Persian proverb says:

$$\text{کَسبِ کمال کن که عزیزِ جہاں شوی}$$

Achieve perfection in some field that you may command the applause of the world.

Hatim of Tai and Nosherwan the Just are universally revered today, because one set the highest standard of generosity, and the other exhibited legendary standards of justice. Those who reach great heights in worthy fields of human endeavour are ever remembered with love and reverence. It is not necessary that we must ourselves share in the particular attributes which have made anyone great; excellence, wherever we find it, draws a spontaneous admiration and love. That is why we admire and love many who lived and died centuries ago. We have an inner compulsion to love perfection, and are emotionally captivated by high standards of goodness.

Now simple reflection will show that ultimate perfection is to be found only in the divine being. We can study any one of His attributes; in each case we will find perfection that surpasses our understanding. Can we do anything but wonder at Him, the Creator, the sustainer, the compassionate, the sovereign, the all-powerful, the all-knowing? Can we contemplate without utter humility how He brought the universe into existence from nothing, and endowed it with its perfect balance?

كردى دوجهاں عياں زقدرت

بے مادّه و بے نيازِ انصار

Both worlds – here and hereafter –
didst thou create,
with thine own unique power,
with no matter pre-existing,
and nobody else helping.

ماه را نيست طاقتِ ايں كار

كه بتابد بروز چوں احرار

نيز خورشيد را نه يارائے

كه نهد بر سرير شب پائے

The moon has no power to shine
during the day:
so is the sun unable
to step on night's throne.

In the astonishing vastness of space, look at the heavenly
bodies, their staggering size, their number, their mutual
distances! How they remain suspended without support, in
constant movement along appointed orbits! And God only knows
since when! If you want details, pick up a simple primer on
astronomy and learn of the wonders which fill the space around
us in every direction. Then turn your gaze downwards from the
heavens to the earth our abode. Compared to the universe, our
earth is but a speck of dust, and yet a knowledge of its dazzling
perfection will send you into ecstasies of acclamation. Examine
anything that exists on this earth and you will behold everywhere
the breath-taking perfection of the Creator of the universe. Study
any field of knowledge and gaze in any direction; in everything
and everywhere are exhibited the unparalleled wisdom, and the

unsurpassed omnipotence of the Lord. The humble and the mighty, the small and the large; all lie in His grasp. Whether we look at a super-star, or see the wing of a tiny insect, the more we learn about them, the more are we overpowered with awe and wonder. The earth, the seas, the mountains, the trees, the stones, the minerals, the plants, our own selves, and all that exists to the farthest reaches of space, one and all bear eloquent witness to the perfect sagacity of the Lord of the universe.

هر ذرّه فشاند از تو نُورے        هر قطره براند از تو انہار

ہر سُوز عجائبِ تو شورے        ہر جا ز غرائبِ تو اذکار

Each particle of matter –
a centre for the diffusion of Thy Light,
each drop of water –
a centre for emitting
waves of Thy grace.

Everywhere they praise
Thy supernatural powers;
everywhere they discuss
the wonders Thou hast created.

According to knowledgeable scientists, there are far more elementary particles in a speck of dust than all the heavenly bodies in the universe. These elementary particles combine with each other under laws of such amazing complexity that our present knowledge of them is very meagre. But even so, we can see clearly that our existing mathematics and algebra are utterly inadequate for a proper comprehension of these laws.

نہیں دیکھا ابھی تم نے مرے محبوب کا چہرہ    جو دیکھو گے تمہارے علم کی پردہ دری ہوگی

> You have seen not yet
> the face of my love:
> when you do you'll find
> your ignorance badly exposed.

Forget the details. Only think how many generations of human beings – generations of this single species of mammals – have come into the world since the world began.

از عدم تا سوئے ہستی ہر زماں    ہست یا رب کاروال در کاروان

> From non-existence to existence
> move pageant after pageant every moment.

The most wonderful thing about these generations of multitudes is that every single individual among them is different from every other single individual. The fact of individual differences is not confined to the human species. It is universal. One particle of sand is different from all the other particles of sand. One leaf on the same tree is different from every other leaf. The lines on each leaf are different from the lines on every other leaf of the same tree. In the same way, the lines on one man's hands are different from everyone else's. And drops of rainwater! Each drop is different, and so is each snowflake, an individual!

Then there is the soil. Same soil, but what different kinds of vegetables, fruits, flowers, cereals, can grow on it. Both sugarcane and colocynth, one most sweet, the other most bitter, on the same soil!

The whole world – whatever is in it and whatever keeps happening on it under laws sanctioned by Our Creator – is wonderful to the extreme. Scientific disciplines are only a search into the wonders we owe to our Creator. Those who know what the scientists do and how they go about their researches know that all sciences taken together are like an ocean, dimensions of which we cannot measure, the ends of which we cannot reach.

علم دریائیست بے حد و کنار        طالب علم است غوّاص بحار

گر هزاران سال باشد عمرِ اُو        اُو نگردد سیر خود از جستجُو

Knowledge, is an ocean without limit,
seeker of knowledge, a diver
a thousand years may he be diving,
unquenched remains his thirst.

The Holy Quran hints at this great point in this verse:

قُلْ لَّوْ كَانَ الْبَحْرُ مِدَادًا لِّكَلِمَاتِ رَبِّي لَنَفِدَ الْبَحْرُ قَبْلَ أَنْ تَنْفَدَ
كَلِمَاتُ رَبِّي وَلَوْ جِئْنَا بِمِثْلِهِ مَدَدًا۔

Say, 'If ocean became ink
for the words of my Lord, surely
the ocean would be emptied before
the words of my Lord came to an end,
even though we brought the like
thereof as further help' (18:110).

Here the wonderful work of which our Creator is the author is
described in the Quran's own unique way. Search for knowledge
brings to light this supreme reality. At every stage we arrive at
in our search the feeling that arises uppermost in our minds is
that what we know is little or nothing compared with what we
have yet to know. There is no comparison between the known
and the unknown. Progress in human knowledge keeps
presenting this scene to us again and again:

معلوم مم شد که هیچ معلوم نہ شد

What I came to know was this,
that there was nothing
I really knew.

And the poet Zauq has said the same thing in his beautiful
style:

اس جہل کا ہے ذوق ٹھکانا پکھ بھی

دانش نے کیا دل کو نہ دانا کچھ بھی

ہم جانتے تھے علم سے کچھ جانیں گے

جانا تو یہ جانا کہ نہ جانا کچھ بھی

This ignorance, Oh Zauq!
has it any limit?
Wisdom makes us no wiser:
we expected much from knowledge,
it has made us aware
only of our ignorance.

If, in short, you look for perfection, you will find it only in
God almighty, our Creator. The Holy Quran invites us to ponder
over ourselves and our worlds, the many worlds. It is impossible
we should ponder and yet our hearts should not be moved by
love – love of the Perfect One, Whose powerful hand has created
this wonderful universe. To love perfection is of the essence of
the nature of man.

There is a moral here for those who deny there is such a thing
as love of God: Why does the Holy Quran invite us again and
again to ponder over the evidences of the perfection and power
of the Originator of the heavens and the earth – that lie before
us? Why this repeated invitation, this appeal? Is it not because

God wants to kindle the flame of love in our hearts? Awareness – true awareness – of perfection anywhere is bound to create in our hearts love of Him Who is perfection personified:

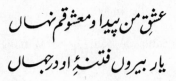

My throbs are surging but my Beloved
invisible;
my friend is away –
yet His beauty is all pervasive.

# XXI

The fourth inspiration of love is self-love. Everyone loves himself. Everyone wants his own perfection and advancement, and dreads his own decline and destruction. We also love our relations and friends. We desire their progress and prestige; for we think of their success and renown as if they were our own. The more their power, influence, wealth, and splendour the more will be our fame and eminence. Our love for them is only another manifestation of our love for ourselves. To love ourselves, and not love our Creator, who is the source of our existence, and of all our progress and excellence would be like worshipping its warmth, but hating the sun. Or like wanting its shade, but running away from the tree which provides it. Our self-love and our longing to live and to prosper involve an inherent urge to love our Creator. He gave us life, and sustenance. He satisfies all our needs. He created our universe with so much beauty, lustre and adornment, and so much for our joy and comfort. He made everything in the world subservient to our good. He did not do this for selfish reasons, only from His graciousness towards us!

من نہ کردم خلق تا سُودے کنم
بلکہ تا بر بندگاں جُودے کنم

This world I did not make
to benefit Me;
rather 'twas to shower grace
on mankind.

That we should pass by such infinite beneficence and grace,

and take no notice of it, is proof of our own ignorance and ingratitude. Is it not?

# XXII

Motives of love we have considered. We have shown that given those motives and springs, the only One really worthy of our love is God. No other, not to that extent, at least. We have drawn on common wisdom and common reason. Now let us turn to the Holy Quran and the Hadith. What have these books to tell us about the subject? Man, it is true, is bound to love God. Does God love man in return? We will see that God's love for man is clearly proved and promised. In the Holy Quran, God describes Himself as the One most approving, the One most understanding:

$$\text{وَاللّٰهُ شَكُوْرٌ حَلِيْمٌ}$$

And Allah is Most Appreciating, Forbearing (64:18).

Of such a being – the One readiest to approve, understand and appreciate – we cannot have the least doubt that He will respond to our love by His. A storm of love in man's heart, but no response to it by God – this is impossible. To have any doubts on this would be senseless, wrong:

$$\text{خدا پر تو پھر یہ گماں غیب ہے کہ وُہ راحم و عالم الغیب ہے}$$

This distrust of God, is a failing.

For Gracious is He,
and knows the Unseen.

Let us first put together passages of the Holy Quran which bear on man's love for God. The passages are many. Again and again we are told that the relationship that subsists between God and man is a relationship of love. Our Deity is not to be worshipped only, but to be loved. He is our real and true love. Let us look at the passages:

وَمِنَ النَّاسِ مَنْ يَتَّخِذُ مِنْ دُوْنِ اللّٰهِ اَنْدَادًا يُّحِبُّوْنَهُمْ كَحُبِّ اللّٰهِ ۖ وَالَّذِيْنَ اٰمَنُوْۤا اَشَدُّ حُبًّا لِّلّٰهِ ۖ

There are men who go for other deities, hold them equal to Allah and begin to give them love which they should only give to Allah. This is not the way of true believers. True believers love Allah the most (2:165).

قُلْ اِنْ كُنْتُمْ تُحِبُّوْنَ اللّٰهَ فَاتَّبِعُوْنِيْ يُحْبِبْكُمُ اللّٰهُ وَيَغْفِرْ لَكُمْ ذُنُوْبَكُمْ ۖ وَاللّٰهُ غَفُوْرٌ رَّحِيْمٌ ۖ

The Holy Prophet is told to tell others this: Say, 'If you love Allah, follow me: then will Allah love you and forgive you your faults, And Allah is Most Forgiving, Merciful.' (3:32)

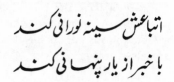

To follow him,
is to light one's heart;
it takes us near Him –
Who lives apart.

The Holy Quran tells us again and again that belief in God inevitably means love of God.

يَاۤيَّهَا الَّذِيْنَ اٰمَنُوْا مَنْ يَّرْتَدَّ مِنْكُمْ عَنْ دِيْنِهٖ فَسَوْفَ يَأْتِى اللّٰهُ بِقَوْمٍ يُّحِبُّهُمْ وَيُحِبُّوْنَهٗ ـ

O believers, whosoever turns away from his faith, Allah will assuredly bring a people whom He loves and who love Him (5:55).

How is man to go about loving God? What practical steps is he to take? Thus:

وَاٰتَى الْمَالَ عَلٰى حُبِّهٖ

... and spends his wealth out of love for Him (2:178). And then:

وَيُطْعِمُوْنَ الطَّعَامَ عَلٰى حُبِّهٖ مِسْكِيْنًا وَّيَتِيْمًا وَّاَسِيْرًا ٭ اِنَّمَا نُطْعِمُكُمْ لِوَجْهِ اللّٰهِ لَا نُرِيْدُ مِنْكُمْ جَزَآءً وَّلَا شُكُوْرًا ٭

They give food, for the love of Him, to the needy, the orphan, the captive: We feed you only for the sake of God – We desire no return, no thanks (76:9).

وَالَّذِيْنَ اٰمَنُوْا اَشَدُّ حُبًّا لِّلّٰهِ ـ

But those who believe are stronger in their love of Allah (2:162).

And

اِنَّ الَّذِيْنَ اٰمَنُوْا وَعَمِلُوا الصّٰلِحٰتِ سَيَجْعَلُ لَهُمُ الرَّحْمٰنُ وُدًّا ٥

Surely those who believe and do righteous deeds – unto them the Most Gracious Lord shall tender the gift of love (19:97).

Now let us enumerate the passages of the Holy Book which

speak pointedly of God's love for man and also tell us what
different kinds of men does God love:

$$اللهُ يُحِبُّ الْمُحْسِنِينَ ۔$$

Allah loves those with goodwill towards others (3:149).

$$إِنَّ اللهَ يُحِبُّ التَّوَّابِينَ ۔$$

Allah loves those who incline towards Him (2:223).

$$وَ يُحِبُّ الْمُتَطَهِّرِينَ ۔$$

Allah loves those who are clean of heart (2:223).

$$إِنَّ اللهَ يُحِبُّ الْمُتَوَكِّلِينَ$$

Allah loves those who put their trust in Him (3:160).

$$إِنَّ اللهَ يُحِبُّ الْمُتَّقِينَ ۔$$

Allah loves those who fear Him (3:77).

$$إِنَّ اللهَ يُحِبُّ الَّذِينَ يُقَاتِلُونَ فِي سَبِيلِهِ ۔$$

Allah loves those who are ready to fight in His cause (61:5).

$$وَاللهُ يُحِبُّ الصَّابِرِينَ$$

Allah loves those who prove steadfast in trials (3:135).

What eloquent and transparent affirmations do we have here
of God's love for man! Persuasive, too. Not the least doubt is left
that God loves man and that it is man's obligation to love God.

Of the attributes of God the two which come first to our notice,
on opening the Holy Book, are the attributes of *Rahman* and
*Rahim*, attributes of mercy – mercy of two kinds, mercy which

comes of unearned beneficence and mercy which brings abundant return for anything we are able to do.

Then we have it in the Holy Quran.

قُلِ ادْعُوا اللّٰهَ أَوِ ادْعُوا الرَّحْمٰنَ أَيًّامَّا تَدْعُوا فَلَـهُ الْأَسْمَآءُ الْحُسْنٰى ۔

Say, call upon Allah, or call upon the Most Gracious Lord,
whomsoever you call upon, to Him belong the Names, Most
Beautiful (17:111).

That is, Allah, think of Him as the deity worthy of worship
or as the gracious One to Whom you must feel grateful. He is
the possessor of all the best and the most beautiful names.

The Bismillah so well known and so frequently met with in
the Holy Quran, viz. 'In the Name of Allah, the Most Gracious,
the Ever Merciful', points to the same thing.

God is loving, merciful, concerned. The attributes *Rahman* and
*Rahim* (besides occurring in the Bismillah) occur more than fifty
times in other places in the Holy Book. In the Sura Baruj we
have the name *Al-Wadud*, usually translated as 'one loved' or
'lovely'. Another name is *Wali*, which means 'Friend' or
'Companion', or 'Comrade'.

If we look at the long list of the attributes (names of God)
mentioned in the Holy Quran and Hadith, we will find that a
greater number of them bear on God's mercy, grace, concern
and love. Why this should be so is obvious. The attribute of
mercy is a root attribute, the mother of all attributes, so we may
say the attribute of mercy is at work all the time in the world.
True, we also have the attribute of wrath. But this also stems
from the root-attribute of mercy. Wrath is not a basic attribute,
not one of the personal names of God. If there is no rebellion,
no disobedience among men, there will be no occasion for divine
wrath. But why forget the other names of God mentioned in
the Quran and Hadith. *Ghaffur*, for instance, the dispenser of
forgiveness, *Ghaffar*, or the great forgiver, *Salam*, the dispenser of
peace. There is also the name *Al-Afw*, one who writes off our
mistakes, our misdeeds, *Al-Wahhab*, the donor, *Al-Hakim*, the

tolerant, *Al-Sabur*, the Patient, one who overlooks unmannerli-
ness, rudeness, *Al-Tawwab*, one who turns to us again and again
with mercy, *Al-Barru*, the ultimate Good, nothing but good. The
names of God, in sum, are names of mercy, of grace, of love, of
magnanimity, of *Rahmaniyat, Rahimiyat*. Let us have a special look
at hints on the nature of God which we find in the Hadith,
traditions or sayings, traced ultimately to the Holy Prophet (on
whom be peace).

$$ أَحِبُّوا اللهَ لِمَا يَغْدُوكُمْ بِهِ مِنْ نِعْمَتِهِ وَأَحِبُّوْنِيْ لِحُبِّ اللهِ $$
(ترمذي بروايت ابن عباس)

Love God, the Holy Prophet said, because He keeps His favour
on you every morn that dawns. And love me because God
loves me (Tirmidhi).

Love of God is one of the essential ingredients of belief in God.
A man asked, 'What is belief?' The Holy Prophet replied, 'To
love God and the Prophet more than anything else.' In the
traditional books of Bukhari and Muslim (according to Anas)
we are told that the Holy Prophet said:

$$ لَا يُؤْمِنُ أَحَدُكُمْ حَتّى يَكُونَ اللهُ وَرَسُوْلُهُ أَحَبَّ إِلَيْهِ مِمَّا سِوَاهُمَا۔ $$

No one really believes unless God and the Prophet are held
above everything other than God and the Prophet, in the
matter of love and regard.

The prayers the Holy Prophet taught us are accented with the
duty and obligation of love. For instance, he taught us to pray
like this:

اَللّٰهُمَّ ارْزُقْنِيْ حُبَّكَ وَحُبَّ مَنْ اَحَبَّكَ وَحُبَّ مَا يُقَرِّبُنِيْ اِلٰى حُبِّكَ
وَاجْعَلْ حُبَّكَ اَحَبَّ اِلَىَّ مِنَ الْمَاۤءِ الْبَارِدِهِ ـ (ترمذى حاكم)

God, give me Your love and give me the love of those who
love You, and the love of things which bring me near to You,
and make for me my love for You sweeter and cooler than the
sweetest and coolest drink of water (Tirmidhi).

Another prayer runs like this:

اَللّٰهُمَّ ارْزُقْنِيْ حُبَّكَ وَحُبَّ مَنْ يَّنْفَعُنِيْ فِيْ حُبِّكَ ـ (ترمذى)

O Allah, give to me
Thy love and the
love of those of use
to me in my love of Thee (Tirmidhi).

An Arab of the desert came to the Holy Prophet and said:

O Prophet of God, I have no deeds to show, neither prayers,
nor fasts, nor any acts of charity. My capital, if I have any, is
the love of God and the Prophet, nothing else. The Holy
Prophet replied

اَلْمَرْءُ مَعَ مَنْ اَحَبَّ ؔ

Be of good cheer for the law is everyone will find himself in
the company of those whom he loves.

Anas says, I have not seen Muslims pleased more with
anything else, after their faith in Islam.

In the course of a battle panic reigned on all sides. Mothers
had become separated from children, brothers from brothers. A
mother, frantic with fear lest she had lost her child, would pick
up every child she met and hold it up to herself, feed it with her
milk. The Holy Prophet – mercy unto all – sighted her and
turned to his companions and said, 'Look at this woman, and at

her concern. Would she hurl into a blazing fire her own child, with her own hands?' The companions said, 'No, it's impossible.' The Holy Prophet said, 'You agree, therefore, that this woman, this mother, could not love her child more. But I tell you God loves His servants much more than this mother loves her child' (Bukhari).

It is also reported that the Holy Prophet was returning from a battle when a woman holding her child came up to him and asked, 'Prophet of God, tell me, does not God love His creatures more than a mother loves her children?' 'Yes', said the Holy Prophet, 'most certainly He does.' 'Would a mother, then, hurl her child into hell, with her hands?' The Holy Prophet was moved and could not speak. Then raising his head said, 'God punishes only those, who out of disloyalty, begin to talk of more than One God' (Nasai).

Then we are told that the Holy Prophet, friend and beloved of God, was sitting, a few others with him. A companion came to join in who had with him a mother-bird with her brood, wrapped in a piece of cloth. He said, 'Prophet of God, I found these little birds on a bush and picked them up in this cloth. As soon as I did this the mother-bird began to hover over my head. I opened the cloth a little. At once the mother dropped on her young'. The Holy Prophet said, 'Are you surprised at a mother's love for her offspring? By Allah Who has sent me with truth, I say this, that Allah's love for His creatures is much greater than this mother's love for her off-spring' (Mishkat).

These citations from the Holy Quran and Hadith are enough to show how great is Allah's love for His creatures. They also show that His creatures, who understand and know, love Allah, their Creator. Those who are not impressed by this spectacle and continue to hold it in suspicion should ponder and think. The relation between God and man is not – cannot be – the dry, lifeless relation of master and servant, commands on one side, obedience and submission on the other. No, it is much more than that. Certainly love has logical and psychological priority over submission. Love comes first, then comes submission.

At the same time we must remember that ordinary analogies

do not help where the object is to understand God. God is unique.

$$لَيْسَ كَمِثْلِهِ شَيْءٌ$$

There is nothing like Him.

So the relationship of love between God and man is also unique, different from ordinary human relations. God's love for man has only a similarity with man's love for men. It is analogous only. When God loves a man it is His dealings with the man loved that we refer to. The dealings are the dealings of the divine love. So is God's anger expressed in dealings appropriate to the divine being. When God is angry with any of his men, again the situation is only analogous to a corresponding human situation. Remember analogous, not identical. Because there is a difference. When one man is angry with another the anger makes the angry man unhappy. The fit of anger has its repercussions. Tranquillity and peace of mind are gone at least for the time being. God's anger is different. His anger has no repercussion for God Himself. He is Holy, free from such weaknesses. Men disobey and earn the anger of God. But this makes no difference to Divine peace. Divine anger results in punishment. But this is only a way of putting it. The punishment is earned. It is the natural consequence of a misdeed. God's part is only to let the misdoer see what the misdeed has brought on him.

# XXIII

A question may yet be asked. The descriptions of hell in the Quran, and the apparently strong language used, do not seem to fit in with our image of the God of mercy – *Al-Rahman*. The answer is, look carefully at the words used. There is no verse in the Quran which says that God is pleased when He punishes. Nor is He like worldly despots with powers of life and death over men who punish when they are displeased and reward when they are pleased. This is arbitrary behaviour appropriate to human despots. Not to the God of the Holy Quran. The Quran has a philosophy of punishment and reward. The hell and paradise of the Holy Quran are a part of this philosophy. The whole matter is full of wisdom, determined in fact, by the requirements of nature. It fits in beautifully with the nature – the God-given nature – of man. Everything is endowed with a nature, a character appropriate to it. This nature confers certain properties on its possessor. Fire burns, water cools, poison kills, its antidote saves life. So, there is nothing in the world without its own appointed properties. Without this order of properties – their effects and repercussions – this world and all that it contains would have been sheer confusion. Everything would have been in a state of permanent disarray. Supposing we had wanted to warm something. We could not have trusted fire to yield the expected heat to warm the thing as we wanted. Maybe fire would begin to behave in quite a strange, unexpected manner. Could life have had a smooth and reliable course in such a case? Could we have executed our plans?

That things have certain appointed properties, that these properties are reliable, gives us an orderly world, a world ruled by law and wisdom. Except for such orderliness, we could have had no life worth living, no possibilities of growth and development, and no progress.

So, here we are, just as law – the law of properties, of causes and effects – rules the world of matter, so does it rule the world of mind and morals. Good deeds have good properties, good effects, good repercussions. So have bad deeds, bad properties, bad effects, bad repercussions. The world of matter could not have been what it is without the law of properties and their consequences. The world of morals also would have lost its significance without such a law. Fancy what would have been the case, if good deeds had come to have bad consequences and bad deeds, good consequences. We could have trusted neither good deeds nor bad. We would have failed to make head or tail of either. Our deeds would have lost all meaning.

The Garden and the Gehenna, described pictorially and repeatedly in the Holy Quran, have just this meaning. The descriptions embody the law or laws which govern morals, good and bad actions, and their natural good and bad consequences. Good that results from good works is called *Thawab* ('spiritual reward'). The evil that results from evil works is called *Azab* ('spiritual punishment'). Spiritual rewards with the appropriate metaphors used for them in the description of the Quran, belong to paradise, the Garden of hereafter promised in the Quran. Spiritual punishment belongs to the Gehenna also promised in the Quran. What the Garden and the Gehenna are, in fact, nobody would know, not in this world. We have explained this before. The true nature of these states or places or institutions is above our understanding and defeats any descriptions we can give for them. We can say with certainty that the descriptions of the Gehenna are descriptions of the consequences of evil choices, evil actions. Why are the descriptions repeated? To serve as warning at every step, at every point of decision, of choice. And what is this but a fulfilment or a requirement of the mercy of God? At every point, at every step, the choice of right action, as well as the avoidance of wrong action, is possible. A reminder is called for, therefore, and is given appropriately wheresoever it is required, so that man may be saved from the bad consequences of bad choices.

If there are still those who will not understand, and cling to an image – a wrong image – of their own making of the God of the Quran, then who is to blame?

$$\text{سُبْحَٰنَ اللّٰهِ رَبِّ الْعَرْشِ عَمَّا يَصِفُونَ ۝}$$

Glorified be Allah – far above their understanding is He (21:23).

Here some people raise another question. Why are not rewards and punishments of the same order as the deeds from which they result. The deed is worship, the reward is the Garden. Worship is one thing and the delights of the Garden quite another. In reply we should remember that common experience furnishes examples of deeds of one kind and rewards of another. A labourer moves stones and bricks but his reward is cash, dollars, pounds or rupees. Physical labour becomes converted into silver. What difficulty is involved in this sort of translation? None at all. If there is no difficulty, why make any difficulty about the rewards and punishments of the hereafter? Especially when we know that in the hereafter, our Creator will manifest His creativity and His concern for man's progress in a new and entirely unique manner. The Holy Quran clearly hints at this.

$$\text{نُنْشِئَكُمْ فِي مَا لَا تَعْلَمُونَ ه}$$

. . . developing you into a form which at present you know not (56:62).

The Garden and Gehenna of the hereafter are the result of human choices and actions in our life here. It therefore seems important and relevant that we turn to the Holy Quran for descriptions of human actions and of how they are recorded and taken into account in the dispensing of consequences.

Says the Holy Quran:

$$\text{فَمَنْ يَعْمَلْ مِثْقَالَ ذَرَّةٍ خَيْرًا يَرَهُ ٥ وَمَنْ يَعْمَلْ مِثْقَالَ ذَرَّةٍ شَرًّا يَرَهُ ه}$$

(الزلزال: ٨ و٩)

Then whoso does an atom's weight of good will see it. And whoso does an atom's weight of evil will also see it (99:8–9).

Again it says

وَوُفِّيَتْ كُلُّ نَفْسٍ مَّا كَسَبَتْ وَهُمْ لَا يُظْلَمُوْنَ ٥ ( آل عمران ٢٥)

And then every soul shall be paid in full what it has earned, and they shall not be wronged (3:25).

And again:

لَا يَلِتْكُمْ مِنْ أَعْمَالِكُمْ شَيْئًا ( حجرات )

He (Allah) will not detract anything from your deeds. Surely Allah is Most Forgiving, Merciful (49:15).

About how our deeds are recorded, the Holy Quran says:

وَكُلَّ إِنْسَانٍ أَلْزَمْنٰهُ طَآئِرَهُ فِيْ عُنُقِهِ ..... إِقْرَأْ كِتَابَكَ كَفٰى بِنَفْسِكَ

الْيَوْمَ عَلَيْكَ حَسِيْبًا ٥ ( بنی اسرائیل : ١٤١-١٥)

And every man's works have we fastened to his neck; and on the Day of Resurrection we shall bring out for him a book which he will find wide open.

Read thy book, Sufficient thy own soul this day as reckoner against thee (17:14–15).

Ponder over this and see how clearly it is laid down that a man's actions are *his*, their recording also is done by *him*, is part of *his* own nature. Nothing to complain, therefore, about the record itself. It is said:

فِيْهِ وَيَقُوْلُوْنَ يٰوَيْلَتَنَا مَالِ هٰذَا الْكِتٰبِ لَا يُغَادِرُ

صَغِيْرَةً وَّلَا كَبِيْرَةً إِلَّا أَحْصٰهَا وَوَجَدُوْا مَا

عَمِلُوْا حَاضِرًا وَلَا يَظْلِمُ رَبُّكَ أَحَدًا ۞

What kind of a book is this! It leaves out nothing small or great but has recorded it (18:50).

In short, every action, big or small, good or bad leaves its trace on the mind of man. The traces thus recorded over a

lifetime begin to speak for themselves in life hereafter. Its quality,
its value and worth, good or bad, not quite evident in this life,
become quite evident in the life to come. There is a difference,
and an important one. During our life here the causal laws,
the properties of things and their consequences are inexorable,
merciless. They allow no exceptions. But in the hereafter the
moral law of rewards and punishments becomes subject to the
unlimited mercy and forgiveness of God. Believers are
commanded never to despair of divine mercy. To despair is to sin.
Hope is held aloft and even sinners are addressed affectionately as
'O My servants'. The form of address is reassuring, morale-
raising. Says God:

قُلْ يَا عِبَادِيَ الَّذِينَ أَسْرَفُوا عَلَى أَنْفُسِهِمْ لَا تَقْنَطُوا مِنْ رَحْمَةِ اللَّهِ
إِنَّ اللَّهَ يَغْفِرُ الذُّنُوبَ جَمِيعًا ﴿الزمر ٥٤﴾

Say, 'O My servants who have committed excesses against
their own souls. Despair not of the mercy of Allah, Surely
Allah forgives all sins! (39:54)
Or,

إِنَّهُ هُوَ الْغَفُورُ الرَّحِيمُ ﴿الزمر﴾

Verily He is Most Forgiving, Merciful (39:54).
Or,

كَتَبَ رَبُّكُمْ عَلَى نَفْسِهِ الرَّحْمَةَ ﴿الأنعام ٥٤﴾

Your Lord has taken it upon Himself to show mercy (6:55).

The most encouraging and sustaining message is contained in
the laconic half-verse

رَحْمَتِي وَسِعَتْ كُلَّ شَيْءٍ

My Mercy encompasseth all things (7:157).

We should need nothing more after this comprehensive and categorical announcement, to feel reassured and optimistic.

God's mercy and forgiveness are available at all times to everyone and everywhere. He says Himself:

يَمْحُوا اللّٰهُ مَا يَشَآءُ وَيُثْبِتُ ۖ وَعِنْدَهٗٓ أُمُّ الْكِتٰبِ

Allah effaces whatever He pleases and establishes whatever He pleases and with Him is the foundation of all commandments (13:40).

In the same strain God announces the merciful law,

إِنَّ الْحَسَنٰتِ يُذْهِبْنَ السَّيِّاٰتِ ۚ ذٰلِكَ ذِكْرٰى لِلذّٰكِرِيْنَ ۞

good works liquidate the effect of evil ones (11:115).

Not only are evils forgiven, their consequences are effaced, all traces removed. And the beauty is that it is within man's competence to earn this blessed result. In the Holy Quran we have a roaring ocean of divine mercy presented to us. But many fail to see it. They have to blame themselves for it.

If your weak vision fails you during the day,
'Tis no fault of the sun.

## XXIV

Love which God has for men and which men naturally have for God, we have shown proof of, from the Holy Quran and the Hadith. The question now remains whether we will ever see this real beloved of all, whether we will ever meet Him. On this we have the following verses of the Holy Quran, clearly promising the much-sought-for meeting:

وُجُوهٌ يَوْمَئِذٍ نَاضِرَةٌ ۞ إِلَى رَبِّهَا نَاظِرَةٌ ۞ (سورة القيامة آيت ٢٣)

Some faces on that day will be bright, looking eagerly towards their Lord (75:23–4).

يَاأَيُّهَا الْإِنْسَانُ إِنَّكَ كَادِحٌ إِلَى رَبِّكَ كَدْحًا فَمُلَاقِيهِ ۞

Thou, O man, art verily labouring towards thy Lord, a hard labouring; then thou art going to meet Him (84:7).

وَقَالُوٓا ءَإِذَا ضَلَلْنَا فِي الْأَرْضِ ءَإِنَّا لَفِي خَلْقٍ جَدِيدٍ ۚ بَلْ هُم بِلِقَآءِ

رَبِّهِمْ كَافِرُونَ ۞

And they say, 'What, when we are lost in the earth, shall we then become a new creation?' Nay, but they are disbelievers in the meeting of the Lord (32:11).

كَلَّآ إِنَّهُمْ عَن رَّبِّهِمْ يَوْمَئِذٍ لَّمَحْجُوبُونَ ۞ ثُمَّ إِنَّهُمْ لَصَالُوا الْجَحِيمِ ۞

Nay, they will surely be debarred from *seeing* their Lord on that day.

Then verily, they will burn in Hell (83:16–17).

اِنَّ الَّذِيْنَ لَا يَرْجُوْنَ لِقَآءَنَا وَرَضُوْا بِالْحَيٰوةِ الدُّنْيَا وَاطْمَاَنُّوْا بِهَا وَالَّذِيْنَ
هُمْ عَنْ اٰيٰتِنَا غٰفِلُوْنَ ٥ اُولٰٓئِكَ مَأْوٰىهُمُ النَّارُ بِمَا كَانُوْا يَكْسِبُوْنَ ٥

Those who look not for the meeting with Us and are content with the life of this world and feel at rest therewith, and those who are heedless of Our Signs – It is those whose abode is Fire, because of what they earned (10:8–9).

فَنَذَرُ الَّذِيْنَ لَا يَرْجُوْنَ لِقَآءَنَا فِيْ طُغْيَانِهِمْ يَعْمَهُوْنَ ٥

But We leave those who look not for the meeting with Us to wander distractedly in their transgression (10:12).

وَالَّذِيْنَ كَفَرُوْا بِاٰيٰتِ اللّٰهِ وَلِقَآئِهٖ اُولٰٓئِكَ يَئِسُوْا مِنْ رَّحْمَتِيْ وَاُولٰٓئِكَ
لَهُمْ عَذَابٌ اَلِيْمٌ ٥

Those who disbelieve in the Signs of Allah and the meeting with Him – it is they who have despaired of My mercy. And they will have a grievous punishment (29:24).

يَعْلَمُوْنَ ظَاهِرًا مِّنَ الْحَيٰوةِ الدُّنْيَا وَهُمْ عَنِ الْاٰخِرَةِ هُمْ غٰفِلُوْنَ ٥
اَوَلَمْ يَتَفَكَّرُوْا فِيْٓ اَنْفُسِهِمْ مَا خَلَقَ اللّٰهُ السَّمٰوٰتِ وَالْاَرْضَ وَمَا بَيْنَهُمَا
اِلَّا بِالْحَقِّ وَاَجَلٍ مُّسَمًّى وَاِنَّ كَثِيْرًا مِّنَ النَّاسِ بِلِقَآئِ رَبِّهِمْ لَكٰفِرُوْنَ ٥

They know only the *outer aspect* of the life of this world, and of the Hereafter they are utterly unmindful.

Do they not reflect in their minds? Allah has not created the heavens and the earth and all that is between the two but in accordance with the requirement of wisdom and for a fixed term. But many men believe not in the meeting of their Lord (30:8–9).

وَاسْتَعِيْنُوْا بِالصَّبْرِ وَالصَّلٰوةِ ۚ وَاِنَّهَا لَكَبِيْرَةٌ اِلَّا عَلَى الْخُشِعِيْنَ ۙ الَّذِيْنَ
يَظُنُّوْنَ اَنَّهُمْ مُّلٰقُوْا رَبِّهِمْ وَاَنَّهُمْ اِلَيْهِ رٰجِعُوْنَ ۟

And seek help with patience and with prayer; and this indeed
is hard except for the humble in spirit.

Who know for certain that they will meet their Lord, and that
to Him will they return (2:46–7).

اُولٰٓئِكَ الَّذِيْنَ كَفَرُوْا بِاٰيٰتِ رَبِّهِمْ وَلِقَآئِهٖ فَحَبِطَتْ اَعْمَالُهُمْ فَلَا نُقِيْمُ
لَهُمْ يَوْمَ الْقِيٰمَةِ وَزْنًا ۟

Those are they who disbelieve in the Signs of their Lord and
in the meeting with Him. So their works are vain, and on the
Day of Resurrection We shall give them no weight (18:106).

اِنَّ الْمُتَّقِيْنَ فِيْ جَنّٰتٍ وَّنَهَرٍ ۙ فِيْ مَقْعَدِ صِدْقٍ عِنْدَ مَلِيْكٍ مُّقْتَدِرٍ

Verily, the righteous will be in the midst of Gardens and
streams, in the seat of truth with an omnipotent King
(54:55–6).

قُلْ اِنَّمَآ اَنَا بَشَرٌ مِّثْلُكُمْ يُوْحٰٓى اِلَيَّ اَنَّمَآ اِلٰهُكُمْ اِلٰهٌ وَّاحِدٌ ۚ فَمَنْ
كَانَ يَرْجُوْا لِقَآءَ رَبِّهٖ فَلْيَعْمَلْ عَمَلًا صَالِحًا وَّلَا يُشْرِكْ بِعِبَادَةِ رَبِّهٖٓ اَحَدًا ۟

Say, 'I am only a man like yourselves; only I have received
the revelation that your God is only One God. So let him who
hopes to meet his Lord do good deeds, and let him associate
no one in the worship of his Lord' (18:111).

And let us never forget what the Holy Prophet himself has
said on this subject:

سَتَرَوْنَ رَبَّكُمْ كَمَا تَرَوْنَ هٰذَا الْقَمَرَ ـ

You will see your Lord as you see the yonder full-moon.

It becomes clear from these citations out of the Holy Quran and the sayings of the Holy Prophet, that the ultimate end of human life is a vision of the Lord God, of His divine beauty and loveliness. The means to this end consist of works pleasing to Him and flowing out of the fullness of love. This is the substance of Islam and of the teachings of Islam. In short there is the ultimate end and there are the means to it. But some would stop at the works. That is, at thoughts and deeds which amount to submission and obedience to the Divine will and person. No more. Submission according to them is *the* substance, *the* end. There is nothing further or beyond. Loving God and being loved by Him, for instance. Then we ask, what is the point in prescribing duties to God and duties to man, to fellow men, that is to say? It is because God, according to them, is like an earthly potentate, in sore need of submission and obedience by men, His serfs? So that, if submission is not forthcoming, the potentate's rule will be in straits and finally come to an end? No, no, God Almighty has no such need, need of worship by men, or their obedience.

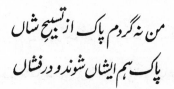

Is it their praises
which make Me Holy?
No, *they* become holy,
who praise Me.

Further citations from the Holy Quran make this point utterly clear. Says the Holy Quran:

مَنْ عَمِلَ صَالِحًا فَلِنَفْسِهِ وَمَنْ اَسَآءَ فَعَلَيْهَا وَمَا رَبُّكَ بِظَلَّامٍ لِلْعَبِيدِه

Whoso does right, it is for his own soul; and whoso does evil,
it will only go against it. And thy Lord is not at all unjust to
His servants (41:47).

And again:

فَاِنَّ اللهَ غَنِيٌّ عَنِ الْعٰلَمِيْنَ ه

The one Self-Sufficient Lord has no need of this universe of
worlds (3:98).

The actions of men do not lie outside: do they?

And yet again:

لَهَا مَا كَسَبَتْ وَعَلَيْهَا مَا اكْتَسَبَتْ

*It* shall have the regard it earns, and *it* shall get the punishment
it incurs (2:287).

To clinch the subject, as it were, we have the specially
authentic saying of the Holy Prophet:

"يَا عِبَادِيْ لَوْ اَنَّ اَوَّلَكُمْ وَاٰخِرَكُمْ وَ اِنْسَكُمْ وَجِنَّكُمْ كَانُوْا عَلٰى اَتْقٰى

قَلْبِ رَجُلٍ وَّاحِدٍ مِنْكُمْ مَا زَادَ فِيْ مُلْكِيْ شَيْئًا ـ يَا عِبَادِيْ لَوْ اَنَّ

اَوَّلَكُمْ وَاٰخِرَكُمْ وَ اِنْسَكُمْ وَجِنَّكُمْ كَانُوْا عَلٰى اَفْجَرِ قَلْبِ رَجُلٍ وَّاحِدٍ

مِنْكُمْ مَا نَقَصَ ذَالِكَ مِنْ مُلْكِيْ شَيْئًا ـ يَا عِبَادِيْ لَوْ اَنَّ اَوَّلَكُمْ وَاٰخِرَكُمْ

وَ اِنْسَكُمْ وَجِنَّكُمْ قَامُوْا فِيْ صَعِيْدٍ وَّاحِدٍ تَسَأَلُوْنِيْ فَاَعْطَيْتُ كُلَّ

اِنْسَانٍ مَسْئَلَتَهُ مَا نَقَصَ ذٰلِكَ مِمَّا عِنْدِيْ ـ اِلَّا كَمَا يَنْقُصُ الْمُحِيْطُ

اِذَا دَخَلَ الْبَحْرَ ـ يَآ عِبَادِیْ اِنَّمَا هِیَ اَعْمَالُكُمْ اُحْصِیْهَا لَكُمْ ثُمَّ

اُوَ فِیْكُمْ اِیَّاهَا ـ فَمَنْ وَجَدَ خَیْرًا فَلْیَحْمِدَ اللهَ وَمَنْ وَجَدَ غَیْرَ

ذٰلِكَ فَلَا یَلُوْمَنَّ اِلَّا نَفْسَهٗ (مسلم من ابی)

God Almighty has said O My men! If all those of you who have lived before you and all those who will come after you, common men as well as leaders among you, were to become as pious and pure as the one most pious and pure among you, even then, no increase would be made to my God-hood. Similarly, O My men, if all those of you who have gone before and all those who will come after you, common men as well as your leaders were to become as vicious as the most vicious among you, no decrease would be made to my God-hood. And O My men! If all those of you who have gone before and all those who are coming later were to assemble together in one place and ask of Me anything they could possibly ask, then even had I given everyone everything he asked for, even then it would make no difference to My Treasures of Mercy and Forgiveness; maybe as little as the amount of water that sticks on the point of a needle dropped in a sea. O My men, it is your own works and their consequences which I keep in safe keeping, on which I keep My eye, and which I make over to you without any addition or subtraction. Therefore, if there is one who finds in his record anything to his credit, let him praise Allah, and if there is one who finds anything to his discredit, let him blame no one but himself (Muslim).

Is any doubt or uncertainty now left on the subject of the ultimate end of our actions? All actions, all works, duties, are intended to promote man's own progress. Fasting is prescribed but only that *you* may become pious; sacrifice is commanded but with the warning that

لَنْ يَنَالَ اللّٰهَ لُحُوْمُهَا وَلَا دِمَآءُهَا وَلٰكِنْ يَنَالُهُ التَّقْوٰى مِنْكُمْ

It is not the blood
or the flesh of the animal
that reaches God—
what reaches Him
is *your* piety (22:28).

Repeated exhortations to piety – *Taqwa* – are to be found in the
Holy Quran.

اِتَّقُوااللّٰهَ

Remain aware of your duty to Allah.

The end of *Taqwa* is closeness to God, to God Himself. Those
who achieve *Taqwa* (piety) are called *Muttaqeen* (the pious). And
the pious are described thus:

وَاعْلَمُوْٓاأَنَّ اللّٰهَ مَعَ الْمُتَّقِيْنَ

Know it for certain that Allah is with the pious (2:195).

وَاللّٰهُ وَلِيُّ الْمُتَّقِيْنَ (جاثيه آيت ٢٠)

Allah is a *friend* of the pious (45:20).

وَالْعَاقِبَةُ لِلْمُتَّقِيْنَ (اعراف ١٢٩)

Only the pious succeed in the end (7:129).

اِنَّ اللّٰهَ يُحِبُّ الْمُتَّقِيْنَ (توبه آيت ٥ ـ ٨)

Surely, Allah loves those who are righteous (9:7).

وَاِنَّ لِلْمُتَّقِيْنَ لَحُسْنَ مَاٰبٍ (ص ـ ٥٠)

Remember, for the pious awaits an excellent resort (36:50).

The upshot now is clear and simple to understand. We seek
closeness to God, that we may achieve the end of our lives. The
way to this is to acquire the qualities, the virtues approved by
God. Good deeds have as their object the attainment of piety,
*Taqwa*. 'Create in you the character – the attributes – of Allah,'
said the Holy Prophet, which means our aim is to try and imitate
the character of God. Imitating God would be to attain closeness
to God. God, the Holy One, finding us patterned on His own
perfect attributes will be pleased with us. Closeness to Him will
be the reward of those who imitate Him.

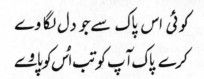

If there be one who will
love the Holy One,
let him cleanse himself –
only thus will he find Him.

We find this the same in worldly relations. Good men join
good men and bad men join bad men. They say 'Birds of a
feather flock together.' God is the holiest of holies. Those who
will be close to Him will have to acquire holiness themselves.
Good deeds done and bad deeds avoided will usher them to His
august presence. We should be able to understand it too. A man
smeared with dirt and filth whose stinking closeness you loathe
cannot have access to a king. In fact, even ordinary men will
run away from his companionship. This being the rule of life,
is it any wonder that evil deeds, deeds disapproved of by God,
deprive you of nearness to God and of a view of His person.
That is why evil deeds are forbidden.

In short the ultimate end for which we live is nearness to God
for the sake of the beatific vision and the blessed and beautiful
presence. On this all are agreed. The means to this end are good
works. On this also we are agreed, but some of us become
involved in the means and begin to confuse the means with the

end. Love of God as the ultimate end is forgotten and dismissed
as a proper end of human life. But if we love not someone, shall
we strive to get anywhere near him? This is what some people
don't seem to understand.

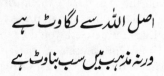

       Attachment to Allah is the real thing
       Should this be not,
       then faith is sheer appearance,
       appearance only.

Naturally one begins to suspect that at bottom it is concern –
exclusive concern – for the life of this world, for political
prosperity, for empire and government, that has brought about
this indifference to God and to love of God.

Islam, they seem to think, came to build and run an empire,
a military state. The institutional prayers and other exercises
prescribed by Islam promote discipline, social cohesion. No
wonder those who like to dismiss love of God from their thinking
lay great stress on the external forms and observances of Islam
and think these exercises most relevant and sufficient for an
Islamic life. But they damage the view of Islam as a unique and
perfect *weltanschauung* for life here and life hereafter. Empire and
government are ends as well – or even better – served by people
and cultures distanced from Islam. Did not Britain create a vast
empire in history, an empire on which the sun did not set? And
yet what spiritual exercises did Britain go through to earn this
empire?

Islam did not come to create an empire. Only – under divine
decree and with divine help – it attained to a measure of political
power and found itself the builder of an empire. And this was to
illustrate its political philosophy as well as to demonstrate the
overall sovereignty of God. This is explicitly stated in the Quran
thus:

Permission to fight is given to those against whom war is made, because they have been wronged, and remember Allah has power to help them (22:40).

But the later generations, dazzled by these conquests, remained blind to the reality in the hearts and souls of the early Muslim conquerors. But those who have drunk deep at the fountain of Islam know the depth of the passionate devotion to God which the Holy Prophet had implanted in the hearts and souls of his companions.

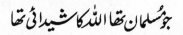

A Muslim true,
was one who loved Allah
through and through.

It could not be otherwise. The cupbearer of the divine elixir had served his followers with the cup, to their fill. They had been taught to remain drunk with this other-worldly love – the seed of which had been sown deep in their hearts.

اسی کے سدا عشق کا دم بھر و تم
اسی کی طلب میں مرو گر مرو تم

Love Him and
live for Him only.

# XXV

If we reflect on the divine purpose in the creation of man, two things become clear. Firstly, to give existence to the non-existent is a supreme quality, and the creation of man has come about from the working of this great attribute of God. Without such creation the requirement could not have been met that all divine attributes should show themselves. Secondly, the divine attributes of being compassionate and merciful had also to be seen in action. There had to be some creature to whom the Almighty would be compassionate and merciful. The Quran reiterates that mankind was created so that it could receive His divine mercy and compassion.

اِلَّا مَنْ رَّحِمَ رَبُّكَ ۚ وَلِذٰلِكَ خَلَقَهُمْ ۗ

Except those on whom thy Lord has had mercy, and for this has He created them (11:120).

But all the Divine attributes are without end and without limits, and that is why, after creating us from humble origins, He ordained that communion with Him would be the aim and purpose of our lives. Thus alone could there be no doubts about his compassion and mercy being limitless. If He had bestowed on us all that is in the heavens and the earth, a yet greater bounty would have still been left outside and withheld. This would have been communion with Him. But as our life's aim is communion with Him, His compassion and mercy are now without limit and without end.

اِس دَرجہ ترقی خاک کو دی      وُہ ہوَشِش میں آکر شوق بنی

اِس شوق کا خود منظورِ نظر      سُبحان اللّٰہ! سُبحان اللّٰہ

This clay
He hath raised so high,
gifted it first with awareness
in quest of Himself,
All praise to Allah,
All glory to Allah.

It is tragic ignorance on our part that we should show great concern, great attraction, for the ephemeral goods of this life – for offspring, for wealth, for power over others, for prestige, for honour, for a good name, for professional excellence – but for our Creator we should have no room in our hearts. We seem to show great concern for the externals of our duty to God, really only the *means* of attaining nearness to Him. But we should yet deny we can have a relationship of love with Him. This is surprising in the extreme. What becomes of our daily prayers in this case? Are not our movements, our pauses, our prostrations, sheer physical processes which we carry through as a habit, under social institutional, or psychological pressures? and fasts mere demonstrations of physical endurance? our pilgrimage a journey undertaken for its excitement, purposeless in any large sense? The Holy Prophet described the daily prayers:

قُرَّةُ عَيْنِيْ فِى الصَّلٰوةِ

Something that lends coolness to my eyes.

Ponder over these words; can physical movements alone – standing erect, hands clasped, half-prostrating, full-prostrating and pauses in between – lend coolness to eyes? No, no, prayer which does not melt the heart is not prayer. It is rather a penalty we pay. True worship comes of love. Worship which is without this ingredient of love is no worship. It is physical labour, physical exercise.

شوق تیرا اگر نہ ہو میری نماز کا امام

میرا قیام بھی حجاب میرا سجود بھی حجاب

If love be not my guide
in prayers,
vain are my reverential postures
and vain my prostrations.

How truly did Yahya b. Maaz say that love as little as a grain
of mustard-seed is worth years and years of prayers said without
the accompaniment of love.

پیشِ حق یک نالہ از روئے نیاز        بہ ز عمرِ بے نیاز اندر نماز

In the presence of the Lord
one cry that rises from the heart
is better than a life-time
of prayer without a heart.

You read accounts of the Holy Prophet, of how he prayed, in
books on his life? Ponder over his example. You have read –
haven't you? – that often, when the Holy Prophet prayed, the
throbbing sobs within his breast would sound like a boiling pot.
Would you still think there is no such thing as love of God,
carrying out commandments, nothing more? But don't forget
that the Holy Prophet's life was a life of love – love of the most
perfect being, our Creator. You know he spent years in the cave
Hira and there, day in and day out, he prayed and prayed.
Could he have done this without being motivated by love? He
had no religious law revealed to him yet. It could not be said
that he was carrying out commandments of any sort, some ritual
prescribed. And then you know what his detractors used to say
when they met and discussed between themselves:

Muhammad is mad,
mad in love,
with his God!

This is what they used to think and say.

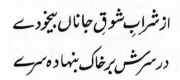

Beside himself with love of God,
thinking only of Him, went about he,
head bowed
in remembrance of Him.

Islam is a religion designed for the nature of man. Our Holy Prophet (on whom be peace) was a perfect model for all human beings in every aspect of their lives. This, in accordance with the famous verse in the Holy Quran:

$$لَكُمْ فِى رَسُوْلِ اللّٰهِ اُسْوَةٌ حَسَنَةٌ$$

For you in the messenger of Allah is a model most perfect (33:22).

On this point of a natural relationship of love between God and man also, the Holy Prophet had to be a perfect model for all of us. And we are not disappointed, as on other dimensions and in other ways; the Holy Prophet (on whom be peace) in the matter of man's love for his Creator, provided a perfect example. His whole life is witness to this.

Those who fight shy of, or respond with a straight rejection to, this idea of a love-relation with God, object that absorption with this idea will destroy our initiative and weaken our interest in the practical problems of life. But exactly this objection is raised by the detractors of religion against religion. They describe religion as an opiate for the masses. But the truth is quite otherwise. True love of God does not make men lazy. It does not send them to cloisters and shrines to live useless, sheltered lives. True religion is not an opiate for the masses making them indolent and unfit for the struggle of life. The life of our Holy Prophet is a practical rebuttal of those charges against our view of God and of our obligation to love Him. If any man living in this world has loved his Creator, then it was Muhammad, the Prophet of the Desert (on whom be peace). But at the same time he was a model of unremitting hard work and continuous struggle against heavy odds. History cannot furnish another example like him. On top of his personal example he gave the world a faith that breathed new life into a people as good as dead.

# XXVI

We have to remember also that man is weak and helpless. He does not know what is in store for him only the next morning. The most powerful men – with all their wealth and following – are, really speaking, weak and helpless. And every man is a bundle of needs, a creature of wants, a *Fakir* (literally, a 'beggar') in the words of the Quran.

$$ اَنْتُمُ الْفُقَرَآءُ اِلَى اللّٰهِ (فاطر۔ آیت ۱۶) $$

it is you who are dependent upon Allah (35:16).

Needy man is well depicted by a poet:

$$ عالم همه درد است و دوا می‌خواهد     از خوانِ کرم برگ و نوا می‌خواهد $$
$$ کس بے حاجت نمی تواند دیدن     درویش غذا شاہ اشتہا می‌خواهد $$

> The world all in pain,
> seeks a potion for relief
> or, from God's bounty,
> anything, anything it can have.
> No one is without need:
> a king needs appetite,
> a dervish his feed.

Thus, on the one hand weakness and helplessness, on the other powers and resources combined with beneficence and charity! And we! we should refuse to turn to Him, to show we are ready to love Him! Is such indifference natural, laudable? A greater misfortune there could not be. The good of both worlds can be ours for the asking. Turning to *this* spring, *this* source. But we turn away, not thinking of a relationship, not of give-and-take, but of love. Yet if we were to love, the gain is to be wholly our own. To hold to His mantle, to walk under this, is where wisdom lies.

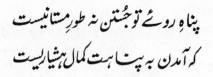

'Tis not insanity to seek
protection with Thee –
'Tis the highest sanity to
seek peace with Thee.

This then is the situation. Our weakness, our helplessness, cries aloud for someone who can help us, lift us out of our helplessness. Our great good fortune is that in the person of our Allah, we already have such a being, such a person. He can afford us the protection we need and seek. And no ordinary protection. He is ready to run towards us, were we to move towards Him in slow steps. He and His mercy beckon us. The Holy Quran tells us so:

فَفِرُّوٓا اِلَى اللّٰهِ ۔

flee ye therefore unto Allah (51:51).

وَسَارِعُوٓا اِلٰى مَغْفِرَةٍ مِّنْ رَّبِّكُمْ ۔

And vie with one another in asking for forgiveness from your Lord (3:134).

To the divine sovereign we have nothing to present but our humility. If we offer our humility, if we abase ourselves, there will be no want of response on the other side. Acceptance of this our meagre and most modest present is already assured. We have only to ask. He is more than ready to give:

زمیں کی طرح جس نے عاجزی وخاکساری کی
خُدا کی رحمتوں نے اُس کو ڈھانپا آسماں ہوکر

Who humbles himself,
like the earth under him,
receives the cover of Mercy
like the sky over him.

If, to our humility and helplessness, we add our sobs, sighs,
the grace from the other side will be abundant. Says Rumi:

اے خنک چشمیکہ اُو گریانِ اُو
وے ہمایوں دل کہ اُو بریانِ اُو
ہر کجا آبِ رواں سبزہ بود
ہر کجا اشکِ رواں رحمت بود
باش چوں دولاب نالاں چشم تر
تا زصحنِ جانت بر روید خضر

The eye will become cool,
that sheds tears for Him;
the heart will become blessed,
that bleeds for Him.
Where water flows
you'll have verdure green,
where tears flow
you'll have Mercy Divine.
Become wet and flowing
like the Persian wheel,
that your life-field may yield
a crop of green.

# INDEX